PRAISE FOR STORM WATCH

*"In **Storm Watch**, Author Charlé Johnson narrates for the reader, a very personal journey into her most vulnerable and victorious moments birthing and caring for a child born with health challenges. This is a treasure of a book that is well-expressed and helps us understand the dynamics, decisions and determination of a faith-filled wife and mother navigating severe weather conditions in her family's life. I have no doubt that readers will experience a true gift and excellent resource for lessons in resilience."*

MICHELLE COLLINS, Ministry Leader, Author, Coach

*"**Storm Watch** is a perfect title for this book, as it gives us a heads-up while preparing us for future storms. I experienced every emotion one can have while reading it, but the biggest emotion I felt was encouragement!"*

SHEP CRAWFORD, Pastor ECM Christian Ministries, Grammy Award-Winning Producer

*"**Storm Watch** is a glimpse into a victor's story, walking through an unexpected time of challenge. She is still able to produce and cultivate an empire that brings great pride to her parents, husband and children."*

MARLENE NORWOOD, MFT

STORM WATCH

All Scripture quotations are taken from The Holy Bible, KJV, MSG

Cover design: *Upscale Media Group*
Interior Layout & Book Coach: *Michelle Collins*
Cover Photographers: *Beverly Lindo-Eyeamshooter (Charlé) and Sloan Studios Dion Sloan (Evan)*
Stylist: *PS Couture Collection by Tomika Hodges*
Hair: *DeeDee Monet*
Makeup Artist: *TeeJay Jones*

This book is dedicated to Evan Christopher Johnson,
my first-born son.

There would be no Storm to Watch had it not been for
you son.

I pray that as you get older you understand the power
of the testimony that was birthed through your life.
I hope that you will be able to see how many lives you
have touched.

There were many people that lost their belief in hope
and faith, until you were born.

May you always walk in your authority and remember
how you survived because you have lived up to your
name of a Warrior.

CONTENTS

FOREWARD

UNDER MY UMBRELLA, I am safe, dry, and protected. Under my umbrella, I am free from the wetness of the rain and the heat of the sun. Under my umbrella, I am a mother of 6; 4 of which I have given birth to. Under my umbrella, I experienced typical pregnancy anticipations, hopes, and journeys. Eagerly, my umbrella equipped me with the gratification of healthy, vibrant, and expectant bundles of joy. Though at times I experienced misty blues, I yet knew that I had the comfort and peace of mind of my trusty covering.

But weather is illusive, and forecasts are subject to sudden change. When least expected, life can throw a curveball that in turn takes a toll. In the face of graying skies, dark clouds, and rolling thunder, can you stand the rain? If nothing else, **'Storm Watch: The Survival. The Sacrifice. The Supernatural.'** reminds us that when the winds are blowing, the rain is pouring and the lightning is flashing, it is your umbrella *(Christ)* that keeps you grounded and firmly rooted.

Storm Watch is personal as it invades private and secret thoughts, feelings, and experiences. It is inspiring, deeply riveting and evokes an array of emotional responses as you read. This book not only pulls at heartstrings but compels you to pull for baby Evan.

Storm Watch reassures you that you are always okay, even in the face of your worst fear. Gear up! Put on your galoshes, throw on your raincoat, and grab your umbrella. Cling close and tight, knowing that you are secure, and protected under your supernatural assurance. Despite the storm, Charlé and the Johnson family are the example of how not to be whisked off and washed away!

Dr. Shalonda K. Crawford,
ThM, PsyD

INTRODUCTION

I would like to take you on the journey of how it all began. It's far from the fairy tale you read in books or see in the movies. However, it is our original love story created by two people, Elton and Charlé Johnson, which cannot be duplicated.

He pursued me for a year before I gave him my full attention. Why? I was busy and I didn't really notice his persistence and determination. At 30 years old, in my mind, I was living it up! I was traveling for work, taking solo trips to Atlanta and Miami just to kick back and exhale from working long hours and leading the dance ministry at my church.

I was a Certified Asbestos Inspector, licensed in the state of California & Nevada, with no set shift hours. I worked early mornings and late nights, graveyard, and swing. I was climbing ladders and scaffolds. I had been on rooftops and crawled in spaces wearing a full-face respirator and head-to-toe disposable suit. I was not interested in small talk while driving from work to rehearsal. I usually used that time to unwind from traffic, get the wrinkles from my mask off my face and choreograph dances in my head, in order to teach the moves upon my arrival.

Throughout the week I would see his occasional Facebook message pop up, *"Hey beautiful"*. I would roll my eyes and proceed to keep working but couldn't deny the fact that I was slightly interested in the person who thought enough of me to ask me, when did I take time out of my busy schedule for myself. The one person that paid attention to details in my Facebook posts. He could read through my sarcasm and subliminal post with no problem.

After playing hard to get for at least a year, I finally let my guard down and our first phone conversation lasted at least an hour and a half. I did not know he talked that much. I saw him around the city at various church events, and he always seemed laid back, and quiet. I said to myself *"This isn't going to work because I talk too much"* but I found out quickly that we were both equally yoked in our gift of gab and ability to make people laugh.

He would always say that he only needed one date with me and after that one date, I would not want to date anyone else. He was correct. Once we went on our very first date to the Prince concert, we became inseparable, and began seeing each other every day. Some days it was breakfast, others it was lunch or dinner. We made sure to connect.

Our favorite date day was on Sundays. We went to different churches, but we would meet up after church on Sundays for dinner or dessert. It did not matter what we chose to satisfy our palettes or cravings, the night always ended with prayer in his car before he walked me to the door. We prayed for each other, we prayed for our families and we prayed for our future.

After only six months of dating, we were engaged. At the time, my dad was in the hospital awaiting a heart transplant. But Elton made sure to ask my dad for my hand in marriage. And on a cold winter night, during the week of Christmas, he proposed to me in front of his assistant, my bonus son, and everyone else at a Beverly Hills, romantically lit restaurant. Was it too soon? Was I ready? I had known him for a whopping six months! In my opinion, we were breaking society's rules. However, we also knew in our guts that we didn't want to be with anyone else and that our relationship was ordained by God.

As daddy's little girl, I was understandably nervous about my father's health. Would he be able to walk me down the aisle, let alone see me walk down the aisle? Two weeks after our proposal, we received a phone call that my dad's new heart was in a helicopter, headed his way and he needed to be prepped for surgery. Thankfully, the surgery was a success on January 6, 2012. After a few weeks of recovery, the surgeon asked my dad *"Mr. Alford, are you ready to walk your daughter down the aisle?"*

I was never like many little girls dreaming about their wedding day. So, prior to getting engaged, I had zero thoughts about flowers, venues, dresses, or color schemes. In fact, I actually messed up my husband's original engagement plans because my parents asked me my ring size and I gave them the wrong size. Yikes! My husband had to get the ring resized and reschedule all of his reservations.

Personally speaking, I thought it was bad luck to try on rings and pick rings out before a proposal. Maybe I made that up in my head. But a month prior to my proposal, we were casually walking in the mall. I did not know he had purchased the ring already. The jeweler asked me to pick out a ring and she smiled after I picked the one I liked. Later, I found out that I had picked out the exact ring that my husband had already purchased.

We picked an August wedding date. To me, August has the perfect wedding weather, and it's the same month my parents and my brother got married. We scheduled our pre-marital counseling, booked our reception venue and we were in full planning mode. 325 invitations were sealed for a church that held a capacity of 800 people, with a 200+ reception list.

We knew we were in love. We knew we wanted to celebrate every moment of our marital bliss with all our family and friends. It was a new journey together as husband and wife. We were thrilled to find a home in a city 50 miles away from where we both grew up. And at that time, it was just us and our dog, Al.

Since my work hours varied from day to day, we spent a lot of time catching up on episodes of Law & Order: SVU and First 48. We also always got a kick out of Lifetime movies. One would ask the other, how we would respond to certain scenarios portrayed in the movies. What would happen if one of us had a long-lost love turned stalker, what if someone kidnapped our children, what if tragedy hit our family so hard and it put one of us in a mental facility? We never discussed the number of kids we wanted. He has a larger family with 8 siblings, and I have a smaller family with one sibling.

Being newly married took some adjustments on my part. I was taking my time learning how to be not only a wife, but also the Pastor's wife of a thriving ministry. I only lived with my parents up until our wedding day. So, I never had to decorate or clean an entire house. Of course, I knew how to cook basic meals to get by, but I only had myself to think about. I had never prepared an entire meal for someone else and for sure not an entire family.

I certainly didn't sit around wondering what kind of mom I would be, and I wasn't into playing house. Maybe I was weird like that. In reflection, I probably was the person my family thought would never get married or never have any children. I was always focused on gymnastics practice, dance rehearsal, ministry, work, and traveling.

In the beginning, I doubted myself at times. There was no book on how to be a Pastor's wife, but plenty on how to be a mom and a wife. But with my crazy schedule, I had no time to read any of them anyway. I think I was just flying by the seat of my pants and compiled everything I saw my mom, aunts, and my sister in-love do. And by the way, where was I supposed to learn how to be a Pastor's wife? Is there a book written about it somewhere? I really did google Pastor Wife's Cliff Notes or Pastor's Wives for Dummies but unfortunately, never found it.

While navigating through this new season, we decided to set appointments for physicals so that by the end of the year we could plan a pregnancy. Lo and behold, I found out at that appointment that I was already pregnant. Although only married for 6 months and still trying to emotionally transition from my parent's house, I was extremely overjoyed to be carrying our first seed. I was painting the picture in my head on what our baby shower would look like. What colors would the nursery be and how I could not wait to start reading baby books as my baby bump grew. More questions like, *what will the first flutters feel like and is that even a real thing? Do people feel the baby moving throughout the pregnancy?* all plagued my mind.

Well, the first trimester was a breeze. We strategically told my family on Mother's Day and we enjoyed making our first social media announcement on Father's Day. We were beyond excited and found pleasure in the fact that the baby's due date was on my birthday. Side bets were made about whether it would be a boy or a girl. I laughed at my husband because he had morning sickness and I did not feel a thing. I enjoyed not having to lift anything and taking nights off cooking in the kitchen. My husband was and still is an amazing teammate.

We were taking trips to "Babies R Us" and "Buy Buy Baby" just to see what the trendy baby items were for the season. When it was time to do our registry, I knew we would be ready. It was all sunshine and rainbows until we found out that the next chapter of our love story was going to include plenty of clouds and lots of rain. Inevitably, we were on *Storm Watch*.

DRESSFORTHE

WEATHER

One of the coldest hits of the 90's was a song by Tony Toni Tone, *"It Never Rains in Southern California"*. As the song relates, the singer was on the East Coast in love with a girl on the West Coast and he was trying to plan a date in California. Unfortunately, he was given the wrong information and he would have been unprepared if he came to see her and did not plan for rainy weather.

We all know that it sometimes rains in California. But the original version of the song was written by Albert Hammond and Mike Hazlewood in 1972. The song talks about the misadventures of a budding singer who wanted his "American Dream" fulfilled by starting from scratch in Los Angeles, CA. The phrase "It never rains in Southern California" is an allusion to the supposed fact that L.A. was the land of opportunities and a sure shot for every newbie in the music business. Sadly, things turn out different, and the line *"it pours.."* refers to the fact that in the end, life in LA treated him harshly.

That was kind of like how I felt. There is an illusion that women feel that they have reached the pinnacle or peak of life when they become married, pregnant, and bring a child into this world. But that was not the case for me and honestly, it isn't the case for many women. Some women struggle with infertility issues, others are birthing children with health challenges and others have complications during the birthing process or have even died giving birth.

I wish more women would be honest about the struggles, hardships, and battles they have faced as wives and mothers. Some women are sick their entire pregnancy. Some develop levels of anxiety and postpartum after the baby is born. If more women were truthful about their dark moments, it would help new mothers know that this journey can take a turn for the worse. That way, women and girls can better prepare their emotions and be dressed properly to weather any storm related to bringing a baby into the world that they may face.

And this false sense of hope that you must be married and have a child before you hit 30 has got to stop. It is challenging finding the right one for you and like a roll of the dice when you get pregnant; you never know what can happen. And you will realize that even more as we dive into my journey.

We were detoured from our excitement and side wiped with grief on a Thursday afternoon. While I was doing laundry, we received a phone call asking us to come into the doctor's office for a visit with the geneticist because we had a test that was red flagged for Down Syndrome and some other conditions that I could not even pronounce at the time.

I hung up the phone and told my husband immediately. It did not sit well with us, so my husband asked me to call the office back and schedule the appointment for that same day. We could not stomach waiting an entire week before hearing the news and full report. They were able to get us an appointment that afternoon right before closing for the day. I am certain we hightailed from our home to the doctor more than 50 miles away. Since we were newly married, I was still in transition of moving all my stuff to our new county. I don't even think I had changed my last name on my important documents yet.

Once in the doctor's office, we were hit with what certainly seemed like a 10-pound bag of bricks, as we were given the list of risks our fetus had. Throughout the rest of the appointment, the genetic counselor began to sound like the teacher on the Charlie Brown cartoon. I could not process anything she was saying. The only line I remember is *"You are both young...you can terminate and try again...the value of this baby's life will be minimal..."*

We left the doctor and headed straight to my parent's home to share this mind-blowing information we had just received. Then we called my husband's aunt and uncle to meet us there so we could share the news with them as well. My husband's mom had passed away years before we met, so we called the closest person who held the matriarch title in his family at the time. After sharing the news with everyone, my father prayed. We decided to keep it a family secret between those in the room, until we had all follow up tests and had a better handle on what was going on.

That next day we did absolutely nothing. Well, I take that back. We did cry like babies, laid in the bed all day, and basically held onto each other. I remember asking my husband *"Why God would do something like this to us. Were we being punished? Were we being punked?"* I was asking him for answers I knew he could not give. But I needed answers because not only have we both served in ministry all our lives, but we were also now the leaders of a ministry serving people and preaching, teaching and showing how to have hope, faith, and how to trust and believe God.

I learned that technology had evolved in such a way that they could see everything via blood tests. To be clear, the risk factors included Down Syndrome, other Chromosome abnormalities, Smith-Lemli-Opitz Syndrome, birth defects, and demise. It was the actual word demise that almost took me out. So, you're telling me I am going to have a child that isn't going to make it?! Does that mean my firstborn will not survive? It looked like my chances of terminating and trying again were better than his chances of living through these risks.

This is when we officially began our **Storm Watch** as our minds were prepped for what was to come. Yet, we had no idea what to expect. We did not know that we had to immediately switch doctors and switch the hospital that he would be born at, see a different specialist once a week to start pinning down and naming conditions.

On another note, we started to figure out which of our friends and family we could share this information with. Who would really be praying for us and who would laugh behind our backs? I am certain that there were quite a few people still scratching their heads, wondering why we got married so fast and wanted to see us fall. There may have even been a few exes on both ends that were disappointed when we got married.

I was thinking, this was the ammunition that they needed. Maybe they thought our relationship was a hoax because we proudly posted our love on social media. This was often looked down upon especially for Pastors and their wives. At that moment, I was so glad to have my spouse because when you get married you should not have to endure storms alone.

But this was also the moment my husband placed the decision to terminate or keep the baby on me. My husband told me that he stood by me no matter what decision I made. I was angry with him! How could he leave such a large burden on me? It was a decision that would change both of our lives forever.

OVERCAST

Overcast means the entire sky is covered in clouds and is usually a dull and gray-looking sky, where the clouds are expected to cover all the surrounding areas. The second trimester was rough, and I did not know what to anticipate day to day, but it reminded me of the sky when it's an overcast day. My emotions and expectations would change daily, and my anxiety remained constant. The appointments really ramped up in the second trimester with seeing specialist after specialist, who all continued to add layers of diagnosis.

The specialists were starting to pinpoint the various conditions. Basically, the fetus was developing slowly with all sorts of congenital birth defects. We went into an appointment to find out the gender of the baby and at that time they could not tell if it was a boy or a girl. The fetus' genitals were compromised. Via the ultrasound, they could not find his stomach and he only had one kidney.

I was nervous and frustrated. Every appointment there was new news or something else they found that was wrong with our baby. The final statement after every appointment was always the same; *"we still have time to terminate and try again. Are you sure you want to continue this pregnancy?"* Sure enough, each appointment, I would sign my name on the dotted line that I was continuing with the pregnancy. I was not ready to give up on my unborn child. I had hope and faith.

The thing about faith is, you do not know where it comes from. It is an invisible gem that holds power to change outcomes. *"Now faith is the substance of things hoped for and the evidence of things not seen."* (Hebrews 11:1) I was hoping for a healthy baby while carrying a baby with compromised and missing body parts. Additionally, our baby was not gaining the proper weight.

The biggest challenge was that after he had a fetal echocardiogram, they found he had transposition of the great vessels. A birth defect of the heart in which the two main arteries carrying blood out of the heart, (the main pulmonary artery and the aorta), are switched in position, or "transposed." It could only be corrected with surgery. According to Children's Cincinnati's Hospital Over 95% of infants successfully undergo surgery in the newborn period. A baby cannot survive without having surgery to get it fixed. The doctors told me they needed me to deliver an 8lb healthy baby in order to perform a successful heart surgery. I began to think *"Where did all of this come from?"* I remember giving a full report of my family history. I really thought it must be genetic. My dad and both of his parents, my grandparents had heart issues, along with one of my aunts and cousin. So, I assumed my side of the family must have been carrying a generational curse of heart disease or heart issues. When I gave the doctor a full rundown of my family history, I also provided dates and diagnosis for each family member. I must have sounded like a scholar being able to recite all the information.

I wondered how my husband felt about that. Is this one of those things you need to discuss before you get married? Do you need to share the health history on both sides of the family so that way you know what you may be passing on to your kids? I was so relieved when the doctor said *"Mrs. Johnson, you are so intelligent, and I am so glad that you know your family history. But what your baby is enduring is random. It has nothing to do with either side of the family."* I held my husband's hand tighter during that visit as I was able exhale on that note.

Since there were so many birth defects and we could not tell the gender, they suggested I get an amniocentesis so that they could rule out some chromosome disorders as well and find out the gender of the baby. There was a long list of risk and side effects. Pre-term labor, leaking fluid, miscarriage, infection, and they could even accidentally poke the baby. I remember thinking in that moment, if the transposition of the arteries does not take him out, the amniocentesis surely will.

Even with all the risk involved, I did agree to the amniocentesis. I thought it would help relieve the stress of whether the baby had SLOS or Down syndrome. That way I could start researching how to care for my child when he arrived. What type of equipment and resources I would need day to day? What type of schools and programs are available to help me with my child?

One thing I was sure of was that I was not giving up on him. I should have known this boy was special in a good way, when he did not move much during appointments like most babies do. However, he tried his best to kick the needle out when they performed the amniocentesis.

I was still working up to this point. And since I was working in a field with environmental hazards, I no longer felt safe. I wanted to take all the precautions I could to protect my baby. As I mentioned, my workday and schedule changed quite often and so did the environment. I could be doing anything from asbestos inspections to mold or microbial clearances in a hospital, lead based paint assessments at a school, or wildfire assessment damage on a home. I am clumsy as well, so I couldn't take any chances falling off of a ladder, or maybe restricting breathing and oxygen to my unborn child, by wearing my respirator for long periods of time.

We decided to have a gender reveal instead of a traditional shower, thinking it would maybe spark some fun surrounding our emotional crisis. The amniocentesis did rule out SLOS and Down's syndrome and revealed the gender which the doctor slid to my mom to tuck away for our gender reveal. But there was a chromosome issue that they could not pinpoint or give a name. The doctors just knew something about it was not right.

The following months and third trimester became interesting as we shared with more family and friends the actual storm that we were facing. Most were supportive and some were unintentionally selfish. I do not think people really understood the severity of what we were enduring. I guess if you have never had to carry a child with missing organs and that could not survive outside of the womb, you really would not understand the stress and anxiety we were up against.

People thought we were joking or withholding information when asked the gender and we would tell them that we do not know. We really did not know and didn't see it as a joke or a laughing matter. All we knew is that in a few months, we would face probably one of the biggest obstacles we have ever had to face as husband and wife.

As a Pastor and Pastor's wife, we normally carry, support and pray for so many people's burdens and problems. I had no time or emotional space for any of that. I had no time for drama. No time for people not speaking to us for things we had forgotten or events we couldn't make it to. We did not even have the energy to fully convey our emotional state to family and friends. We were going through so many changes. The numerous amounts of doctor's visits and the change of the delivery hospital caused us to move back to the Los Angeles area. We never settled in our home in Rialto, CA. I still had unpacked boxes from my parent's house in my new home because we were still honeymooning and getting settled in before I got pregnant.

At this point, I did not know if I was going or coming. My husband was focused on getting us closer to the hospital, closer to our support system and I was talking to my belly every day. *"Hang in there kid." "We are going to make it, kid."* He was not moving enough throughout the day when I would count his kicks. Non-stress testing was a must two to three times a week in the last trimester. They would make me drink cold juice or ice water to wake him up and see how many times he would move in my stomach.

Other than trying to wrap our minds around getting the nursery together, we did have a photo shoot. I wanted to be comfortable, so we rearranged my parent's living room into our own personal photo studio. We dressed up as kids and pretended to emulate an elementary school yard game of who was better, girls or boys. This kicked off our gender reveal theme of team girl or team boy and team pink or team blue. People got a kick out of it when we posted the pictures on social media, not knowing it was just another one of our ploys to distract us from the anxiety and stress of what was to come. Or just one of our ways to laugh to keep from crying about the fact that our baby had severe challenges leading up to the birth.

In late November that year, we tried to get a day of fresh Fall air and go to one of those new dine in movies. "Best Man Holiday" had just come out in theaters and we couldn't wait to see it. I had on my comfy uggs and a maxi dress which was snug enough to show my baby bump, yet comfortable enough to remind myself that my waddle days have arrived. We were in for a rude awakening at the end of the movie.

What was supposed to be a nice time to ourselves ended in me crying like a baby. I was thinking even in this movie, they had a happy ending and were able to hold their brand-new bundle of joy. I thought in my head, "*Lord, please just let it happen for my family.*" That day really messed me up. Also, I then saw a high school classmate on our way out of the theatre. She spoke to me and I barely spoke back trying to gain my composure thinking she would not even understand if I tried to explain to her my emotions from the movie.

At this point, I believed nobody understood what I was going through. I am sure a lot of people cried at the end of that movie. But my tears were for a different reason. I was asked to deliver an 8lb baby (who had already stopped growing at 3 lbs.) so that he can have open heart surgery at birth to live a life that will be minimal due to some random birth defects.

Logically none of it made any sense. The baby was so small inside of me that I could barely feel him move. His moves felt like flutters that you would feel in the early gestational weeks. I was deep in my third trimester and he was only 3 pounds. He had stopped growing in the 8th month of my pregnancy. I began to worry but was steadfast in every attempt to enjoy awaiting his arrival.

The gender reveal was perfect, except for the heat lamps that would not work so we all almost froze to death. Our family and friends surrounded the warehouse walls. There were mini blinged out pink and blue converse chucks everywhere. Since Chuck was my nickname growing up, it was only right to incorporate it into our gender reveal theme. Baby Chuck or Baby EJ was on the way! The support was overwhelming. Our family and friends started to tap into our emotions and realized we were doing our best to enjoy the celebration. But we still inhibited some worry and anxiety surrounding his arrival. The side bets were all in for our final raffle. Was it going to be a boy or a girl? Only my mom and the doctor knew up until this point.

As the blue balloons floated from the box and everyone yelled *"It's a boy!!"* I had no thoughts or cares about the gender. I disappeared emotionally for a second to whisper a simple prayer *"Lord, bless my child."* And then I added, *"Oh and by the way Lord, since it's a boy, you know we are a sports family. If by chance he can't be an athlete because of all of these issues, please bless him to be a talented artist."*

We knew we wanted to go with a name that started with the letter "E". We liked Elliot since our favorite character from "Law and Order SVU" was named Elliot Stabler. But it just did not sit right. We googled more "E" names and Evan just kept popping up. We decided on Evan Christopher Johnson, to represent our initials.

INCLEMENT

WEATHER

We had been preparing our minds for the birth and surgery to immediately follow his arrival. I was able to gather everything I had left within myself, just to become laser focused on keeping myself healthy, so that I could deliver the baby right into the hands of a NICU team and operating staff. On Christmas Eve we went in for what would have been our final consultation before they induced me and prepped for a C-section.

We had discussed the date of induction. Which I was told to report immediately to Kaiser Sunset after church on Sunday December 29, 2013. We laughed at the thought of a potential New year's baby, as induction can take anywhere from two hours to three days. Physicians usually do the consultation first before the exam. After our conversation was complete and she checked the schedule to make sure all specialists and doctors would be ready for Evan's arrival, she began the exam.

In my mind I was already at Sunday, December 29th, the day of my scheduled induction. I was thinking *"How long will labor take? What will this C-section feel like?"* and the ultimate question brewing in my head was, *"how fast will they whisk my new baby away?'* I just wanted to hold him for two minutes or so. *Will he be blue like all the articles I read and traumatized myself about? How soon can I breastfeed? What is this kangaroo and skin to skin stuff moms talk about?* I wanted all of it. *"Lord, please just make it happen for me and my child."*

I was so lost in a daze but not for long because suddenly I heard the doctor say *"Uh oh"* I was fully alert and had my antennas up. She said, "*I'm calling the team and telling them you are on your way now*" Wait, on our way where? She continued *"You won't make it to Sunday. You have lost too much amniotic fluid. The baby has to come out of there."* I thought, *"Lady! It's Christmas Eve! I have stuff to do. I didn't come here for this today."* I knew back at home, my mom had ordered dozens of tamales for me. I was looking forward to going and eating them. Additionally, I had gifts to wrap not to mention my infamous last minute shopping trip.

We then had to place a call to my parents. Of course, the first thing out of my mom's mouth was about how she had just bought my tamales (*yes, lady. I know that*). I told her to just meet us at Kaiser. We called one of our staff members who lived by us at the time and was our designated labor and delivery driver and we headed to Kaiser Sunset. My parents were so excited, supportive, and worried, that they beat us to the hospital. I hadn't even checked in yet but received a call on my cell that I had visitors. At this point I'm all smiles. I have one job to do and that is to deliver this baby, bring him into this world so that they can fix him, and I can take him home and love on him, teach him about loyalty, and of course raise him to be a Raider fan. Or I guess maybe a Cowboys fan, if my husband had his way.

36

The induction process started at 5pm. We began the hurry up and wait game. My dad, mom, wonderful husband, some family, and a host of nurses and doctors were present, just hanging out on Christmas Eve. It was a long day and an even longer night as labor progressed. I was on bed rest, while they monitored the baby so closely. The concern of his heart rate was key.

The Pitocin kicked in and the morphine was kicking too. I could not have too much pain medicine because of his heart condition. I never received an epidural with him. I was going to wait until the last minute. I wanted to give him every chance he had at natural birth. I did not want to taint the process. I asked the nurse if I could go to the restroom one last time. I was really tired of laying in the bed and just wanted to walk around. I did not think it would be a big deal. Plus, they did not think he was strong enough to make it through the birth canal.

But to our surprise, my little walk from the bed to the restroom made me dilate from 3cm to 10cm. it was mayhem and panic! They kicked all my visitors out while my husband helped me wobble back to the bed and after 24hours of labor, more guests and family visits, Evan Christopher Johnson came through the birth canal like the little warrior he is!

It only took four good pushes. He was the cutest and smallest baby that I had ever seen. I was able to hold my 4lb Christmas gift for a good thirty seconds before they took my miracle baby away. I was hoping for at least a minute. But I was so grateful because that thirty to forty-five seconds was way longer than I expected. It made my heart glad. He had a head full of straight black hair, his eyes were wide open, and he looked at everyone in the room.

I could not believe that my parents beat us to the hospital and then turned around and missed the actual moment he was born. They had just pulled up in the driveway at home after spending the night with us and waiting all day and night for his arrival. But back to Baby Evan, who observed everything and everybody, as if to say, *"I'm here! I made it!"* It was our first indication that we had a warrior and a little fighter on our hands.

My brother even swears that Evan winked at him as they rolled him down the hallway to NICU. I had no idea what was happening next. But my Husband was the absolute best running back and forth between NICU to check on any updates with Evan and then back to recovery to check on me. I had to have a small procedure after the delivery. Still can't believe that Evan came out of the womb fine, but my placenta didn't want to deliver. So, I spent the rest of the night in OR and OR recovery.

Through it all, I thought *"My Christmas gift has arrived."* I had never received a gift so special, so precious, so sentimental. Christmas for my family will never be the same.

CATEGORY 5

HURRICANE

According to the National Ocean Services, a hurricane is a type of storm, usually occurring between June and November called "Hurricane Season" but can also occur outside of that time. Hurricanes have categories of winds on a scale of 1 to 5. The higher the category, the greater the hurricane's potential for property damage and lives lost.

One such hurricane was in effect by the name of Hurricane Katrina, when my brother and his wife, Jan got married in August 2005 and we were included as a family on their trip to Jamaica for their honeymoon. When Hurricane Katrina made landfall in the gulf, we were in the pool in Jamaica, enjoying the water aerobics, when large raindrops fell from the sky and thunder sounded throughout the resort, like I had never heard before. The resort staff began to tell us that it was not safe and that we all had to get out of the pool until the storm passed.

We retreated to our rooms and watched on the news the devastation that had occurred in Louisiana, Mississippi and surrounding states. On that trip, that was the only day we stayed in our rooms. It was heartbreaking to watch people sitting on top of buildings, trying to escape the flooded cities or people fleeing to the Superdome for shelter, which was a place I had visited for the ultimate college event "The Bayou Classic" just a year prior.

I knew that after he was born, we had some hurdles to cross, but I never saw half of the storms-hurricanes - coming our way. Our nucleus, close family came to visit on Christmas Day. No one could see Baby Evan though. They weren't upset or anything, they just brought good energy and prayers. Again, my husband was being the best running back and forth from NICU to OR recovery to make sure I was good, and our Christmas gift was thriving. We were in heaven. Our Miracle had arrived on Christmas. He beat some odds. God had smiled on us. I guess it took our minds off of the fact that we had a 4pound baby who had health issues.

Although his stomach was nowhere to be found during the pregnancy, his stomach was found after he was born. That other kidney showed up too, but they were both on the right side. They immediately taught me how to express breast milk. I wanted to change diapers. Take his temperature. Swaddle him up. But I could not do any of that. So, I became what felt like a breast pumping machine. I made sure he had all the milk he needed. This is while being stationed in my postpartum suite missing my baby. I needed just one good glance at him. I wanted to count all of his fingers and toes. See how big he was. And see if he would wink at me like he did my brother. Questions like *"Does he recognize my voice"?* ran through my mind.

He was in NICU for 24 hours and he was transported across the street via ambulance to Children's Hospital Los Angeles to prepare for the next steps. My husband had to ride with him, which was the shortest ambulance ride of his life. I had one job, breast milk and I was committed. Or maybe my nerves were bad, I don't know. We were basking in the ambiance of our Christmas gift that we almost forgot what really lay ahead of us.

The surgical team from Children's Hospital called my suite saying they needed to have a consultation with us regarding his open-heart surgery. I was hoping it was a dream and that it somehow corrected itself during birth. But it was all too real. My 4lb pound newborn baby needed a full open-heart surgery. I do not know what the rules are or the time frame of recovery for postpartum mothers, but I said check me out and take me to my baby. I was so determined to get to him that I totally forgot I had just given birth and had surgery. I could barely walk. I had managed to make it mid-way to the lobby and hallway at CHLA and by then had to request a wheelchair.

The doctors were waiting on us. So, we had to have our meeting before I could see Baby Evan or his new hospital room in his new environment in Cardio Thoracic ICU, a special floor specifically for heart babies. The team was so calm. That helped ease our anxiety a little. They assured us that they perform these surgeries all the time and that Evan would be fine stating that this will be harder on us than it will be for him. They mentioned that Evan was not going to remember most of it. But he would need multiple surgeries throughout his life and that he would most likely require medication for the rest of his life.

They also explained that he was not big enough for them to perform the surgery yet, but they would burst some holes in his heart to buy him some time to gain a little weight. He could survive another few days but would definitely need the surgery in the next week or so. The surgeon went over the list of risk and side effects naming nerve damage, infections, and possible death again. He also needed blood transfusions. They told us that their blood bank is large, but we should call our friends and family to donate blood to keep the blood bank flowing.

By this time, word was out on social media that The Johnsons had a Christmas baby. Posts like The Johnsons had a baby that will not survive. People were calling and texting and posting. It was like an APB went out to all of our friends from elementary, high school, college and the church circuit. People were sending prayers, good vibes, and money for us to eat. People were sharing stories about their nieces and nephews that were heart surgery survivors. Evan's condition was so complex I just could not explain it to the people. In addition, while I appreciated everyone's concern, it just was not everyone's business. I wanted to crawl under a rock and just have my husband and I deal with this huge cloud that surrounded us. My insecurities were creeping in, I did not want to be vulnerable in front of the people.

While waiting on him to gain weight, some of the Pastors in the city wanted to have a prayer service in Evans' honor. That same day, we passed by a conference room. We were going to inquire how to rent it out so we can gather and pray. But our clergy friends beat us to the punch. They were already discussing how they could help us. They told us not to worry about it, and that they would plan it and all they needed us to do was to just show up.

Evan had tubes and fluid lines everywhere. He had the cutest heart shaped cut tape holding his tubes in place on his tiny face. They even gave him his first haircut on the side of his head to insert an iv line there. I was not too thrilled about the patch missing on the side of his head, but at least they saved it in a little baggie for me. I did not know what to do. Was I able to hold my baby with all these cords and lines and machines attached to him? The nurse asked me was I ready? I had no clue what she was talking about.

The nurse began moving wires and cords and machines to prepare me to hold him officially for the first time. He was a few days old and I was ready. He was so tiny and fragile. You could see him struggling to breathe as his little chest looked like it was working overtime. But he smiled and was calm and content. He had a peace that surrounded him. He would look me and my husband dead in the eyes when we talked to him and interacted with him. Maybe my brother was not lying about Evan giving him a wink after he was born.

The clarion call was ultimately made on our behalf by my husband's best friend who also happens to be Evan's Godfather, along with the President of the Baptist Minister's Conference. Pastors, Preachers, their wives, our family, our friends & pretty much the entire city of Los Angeles came together for a night of prayer specifically for Evan. I remember they asked me to not come and to stay home and rest or to stay at the hospital with Evan. Not only was I restless, but I was also a little disobedient. I had to be there. Standing in agreement. Standing in prayer. I needed the people to see my face. I needed another mom to see my faith and to see my strength.

I was right in the middle of the biggest storm of my life, but I was not backing down. I was using every bit of shelter I could find. My village banding together to cover my child is what I needed. I was being strong. A warrior for faith. I was not giving up on my child. The leading Pastors in the city lined the staged and family and friends filled our sanctuary, balcony and overflow. People were parking blocks and blocks away to get there to touch and agree. Some had to turn around and go home because there was no parking. We were given specific instructions to pray for strength, healing, the recovery, among other things.

Before closing out the service, Rev. Melvin Wade Sr., the former pastor of the Mt. Moriah Baptist Church in Los Angeles, gave us the mandate to continue in prayer every day at 6pm. That was the night that Team Evan was born. Team Evan became a group of people, near and far, who were given instructions to intercede for Evan at 6pm everyday. The team checked in on Facebook to let us know that they were on board and praying every day at 6pm and they were all in. Most people knew we had a baby on Christmas Day and he needed some kind of surgery to live. But most did not know all the details.

We sat bedside daily waiting for the surgery date. Exactly one week after the city-wide prayer service, and two days before my 33rd birthday my son endured his first open heart surgery at only two weeks old barely 6 pounds. The night before, I was able to help the nurse give him his first bath. That was the first time I heard his little cry. He fussed at us. He did not like it at all. His voice was so raspy but had such a strong cry. Family and friends lined the cardio thoracic ICU family waiting room. We were only allowed 2-5 people in there per baby, but for Evan we had at least 10-15 people.

I kept my iPad and phone charged so I could listen to the family member's conversation yet tune out to listen to my gospel music. I could not keep up on social media. My Dad and husband served as Evan's publicist. They would alert Team Evan on the status and updates. People were eager to hear when the surgery was complete. They wanted to know if we ate and how I was doing and what could they do to help. People were tapping in with stories about friends and families with babies who had heart surgeries at birth.

Occasionally I had to go pump. I had recorded a video of Evan crying and had one of his blankets with his smell on it to help the milk come down when he was not in my presence. I do not remember eating much. Mainly, just staying hydrated enough to produce milk. Pumping and praying was all I could do. The staff gave us a pager in case we left the hospital. The support was amazing. Even one of my best friends who was a police officer pulled up to the hospital and parked illegally, just to check on the status of the surgery. Although we were at capacity in the waiting room, they had to let her and her partner up because Evan was a serious matter.

After what was 4 hours of surgery, the surgeon then came in with the report we were waiting for. The procedure was complete! The transposition of the great vessels was corrected. However, while in there they noticed some other issues with his heart that they were able to temporarily fix. He was so small and would eventually outgrow whatever patch work they performed on his heart. They told us they would clean him up and then we could see him. They warned us that his chest cavity would still be open. They could not officially close him up until the swelling went down, after a day or so. And he would still be on the breathing machine.

I just prepared myself for the worst. I did not know what my baby was going to look like. I was just ready to see him. Ready to say *"Hi Evan! It's Mommy! Can you hear me? Can you recognize my voice?"* After another hour or so passed, we were able to go in. It was a gut punch. I felt like someone had knocked the wind out of me. All I heard was machines and beeps. His chest was indeed wide open with a thin film over his heart and thoracic cavity to keep infection and germs from getting into his open incision. If you were close enough you could see his insides. The breathing tube was still inserted and helped him to breathe. He had two large tubes inserted on the sides of his chest cavity for fluid drainage.

His nurse was moving swiftly about his room, checking all numbers and fluid levels. She asked if I had a picture of us that we could tape to his crib, so that when he awoke, he would see us. She told us to get ready because the road to recovery is the hardest part. They were slowly weaning him off of machines and medication. He slept most of the time. And within 24 hours, we hit our first bump in the road.

This would be our first sign of permanent damage from the hurricane. Unfortunately, one of the risks of heart surgery is nerve damage. During the surgical procedure, they damaged a nerve where the top of his heart no longer communicated with the bottom of the heart. So his heart was out of rhythm and would not beat long on its own.

During doctor's rounds, they said that we had to meet with the surgeons again because Evan was going to need a pacemaker. Now, this is a space I had been in before. My own dad had a pacemaker and defibrillator years before he had his own heart transplant. My dad's pacemaker drove us crazy. The defibrillator had shocked my dad more than once. I recalled seeing him be knocked down to the ground from the shocks of his defibrillator. I have had to call the paramedics on numerous occasions for my dad. Our local fire station and medic's team had been to my parent's house so many times that they already knew where we kept his medication. I was not thrilled to hear that Evan now needed a foreign object in his tiny body. A pacemaker?! Really?!

So that means Evan cannot walk in front of microwaves and he cannot be tackled or play rough? And to me, the ultimate was my first-born son cannot play or participate in any contact sports at all. When you are raised around sports, you dream of the day you have an athletic child. I know the successes of life are not built on athletics, but it was one of my hopes to see my first male child score one touchdown or shoot one free throw. I could not wait for his Uncle to teach him how to throw or catch. Or for my husband to teach him how to slide into home base. Now, not so likely. They told us that they would give his heart time and maybe after the surgery, the communication may then come back, and he wouldn't need a pacemaker.

We waited it out for a few days to see if the nerves would heal. Meanwhile, everyone was still praying at 6:00 pm daily and checking in on Facebook. However, the damage was done, so seven days after his first open heart surgery, he went in for his second open heart surgery at only three weeks old. His little body had not even healed yet from the first one. He was on so many different medications for pain and bleeding. I was thinking *"Just give us a break please!"* We already made it so far. We crossed over the threshold of him surviving being born and surviving the surgery. I felt like I was the poster child for faith for an entire two weeks and now there's more?

There was a different level of transparency that we began to have with the people. I did not like being that vulnerable. They wanted to know how Evan was doing, how Evan was recovering? Evan became everyone's favorite little warrior. Meanwhile, I was crawling in a shell. I did not want people to know what was going on. I did not want to break, seem weak or crumble behind this. I was taught to always be strong, to hold my head up high and never let the world know when I was getting beat up. The people meant well, and the support was amazing, but my emotions were starting to show, and they could see my heart. I just wanted my son home. I just wanted it to be over.

After a two-hour surgery, Evan was back in his room. He was so tiny that the pacemaker was placed in his lower abdomen. It protruded like a little pack on the side of his body. The wires to his heart were wrapped multiple times in his body, so that as he grew, they would stretch. There were different bandages this time. Not as many tubes, but the look of disgust on his face. He was tired of them bothering him. He would fuss at them every time they came in. The nurses got a kick out of it because they said baby heart patients did not interact much with them. But Evan made sure to let every nurse or doctor know that he was watching them when they entered the room or when they talked to him. He always responded with a facial expression or some sort of body movement.

The next few weeks consisted of late nights and early mornings. We were stationed at uncomfortable positions by the bedside. My husband and I doubled up on the tiny bed they had next to Evan's bed. It was a bed made for one person, but we made it work. We called it "toes to nose". That is the only way we could fit. Our heads on opposite ends of the bed. Sometimes switching to the chair when we would hold him. We were both pros by that point. We knew how to swaddle him around the wires and leave them hanging and attached to all machines. It was quite the system to get up and move around, but we had it down packed. My husband talked with him a lot during this time. They bonded greatly. I didn't talk much. I was always praying silently and having a lot of talks with God.

My husband still had to work. He still showed up for Bible Study and church on Sundays. We were living at the hospital, so he would go push hope and faith to the people and then come right back to the hospital where our hope and faith were being tested. Evan had to learn to eat at the hospital. All his first month milestones happened in the hospital like how to hold our hands, how to suck and how to recognize our voices. I had to learn how to change a diaper with tubes and wires attached everywhere. They were finally able to stop feeding him through a tube and started bottle feeding him the breast milk a little bit at a time. I was able to latch him once after the 2nd surgery, but he was already used to the hospital grade nipples. It did not bother me much. As long as he ate something.

I was still a pumping machine. I had pumping machines at the hospital and everywhere else like at home, my parent's house, and in the car. I would report to Facebook every now and then, dropping little nuggets here and there for the people and Team Evan. But it was mainly to keep me encouraged along the way.

Counting days seemed to be my newest pass time. We wore our weekly parent badges proudly through the hallways of CHLA. We acknowledged parents with a simple head nod in passing. There wasn't much dialogue between parents. The look and nod sufficed as to say, *"You hang in there and so will we"*. On occasion a conversation would break out. The same questions are always asked, how old is your child? How long have you been here? and lastly the one that shifted the atmosphere, when do you get to go home? Some parents would say, *"My child isn't leaving"*. Others, like us were lucky enough to say *"He'll be going home soon"* or *"He'll be going home when he recovers".*

And after 37 days of being born, two open heart surgeries, recovery, collapsed veins, lots of needles and respiratory therapy, blood transfusions, we were indeed going home!! I was able to exhale. Although meteorologists can predict hurricanes, there isn't a way to properly prepare for the damage, nor can you control what the storm damages along the path. I visited Gulfport Mississippi and New Orleans, post Hurricane Katrina. The company I worked for at the time had clients who owned the casinos and hotels. Our job was to assess mold damage from the hurricanes on the remaining floors of the building. Some of the casinos were partially standing. In some cases, the entire east wing was missing, or should I say somewhere floating in the ocean. We would drive by churches where only the balcony remained. Sheets and clothes were scattered throughout trees from nearby homes. Well, I assumed there was a home there because there was a porch and a foundation, although no sign of a structure. The shape of the McDonald's & Chevron signs was still standing but the actual sign was gone.

That is exactly how I felt about this phase of the journey. The damage from this storm left unrepairable emotional scars within us and physical scars for my son. We knew the storm was coming. We did not know how hard it would hit. His transposition of the great vessels was fixed, yet he now had a pacemaker. They said they could not find his stomach while I was pregnant, but it was there when he was born. He was just small with poor weight gain. They said they could not find his left kidney, but it was on the right side.

The geneticist did a very thorough investigation after he was born. They concluded that all of this was because he was missing a piece of his number nine chromosome. There were only eight reported cases in the world. All other children who suffered from this had very similar characteristics and challenges included but not limited to heart issues, low birth weight, hypospadias, & learning disabilities. The one characteristic that Evan didn't share with four of the eight reported cases was physical deformities on his face. It was also too early to know about any learning disability, because that was something we couldn't figure out until he was older.

We didn't know we had some extra coverage or shelter with the pastors and preachers in the city and Team Evan. Some days I felt like that church I saw along the highway in Gulfport Mississippi that was missing the building, but the balcony was still intact. My mind was gone but my body was still intact functioning day to day. So many people held us up in prayer, on days we could not pray for ourselves. I am forever grateful for those people. I am grateful for my parents who were at the hospital sitting bedside during doctor's rounds with us as much as they could. My parents tried to give us breaks to go home and refresh and repack for the week. Our friends, Evan's Godparents, the Hiltons, who had a similar situation with their daughter at the same time as us. We never left each other hanging. Our shelter during that hurricane was God, our family, our friends, and the City of Los Angeles. Thank you and thank God.

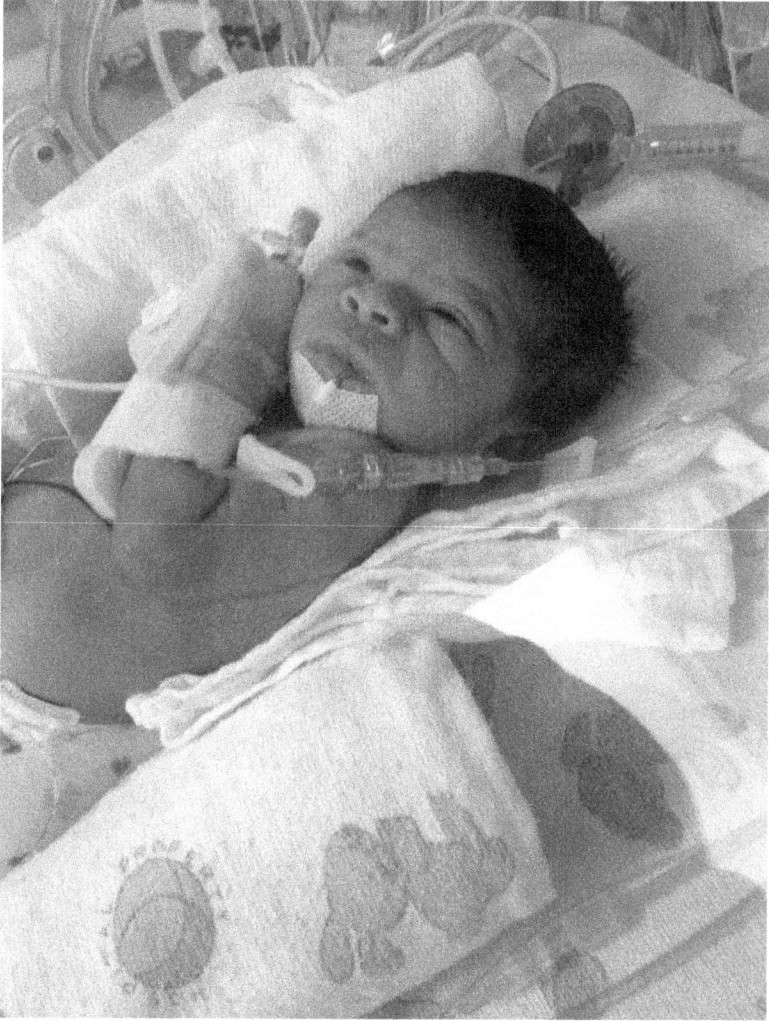

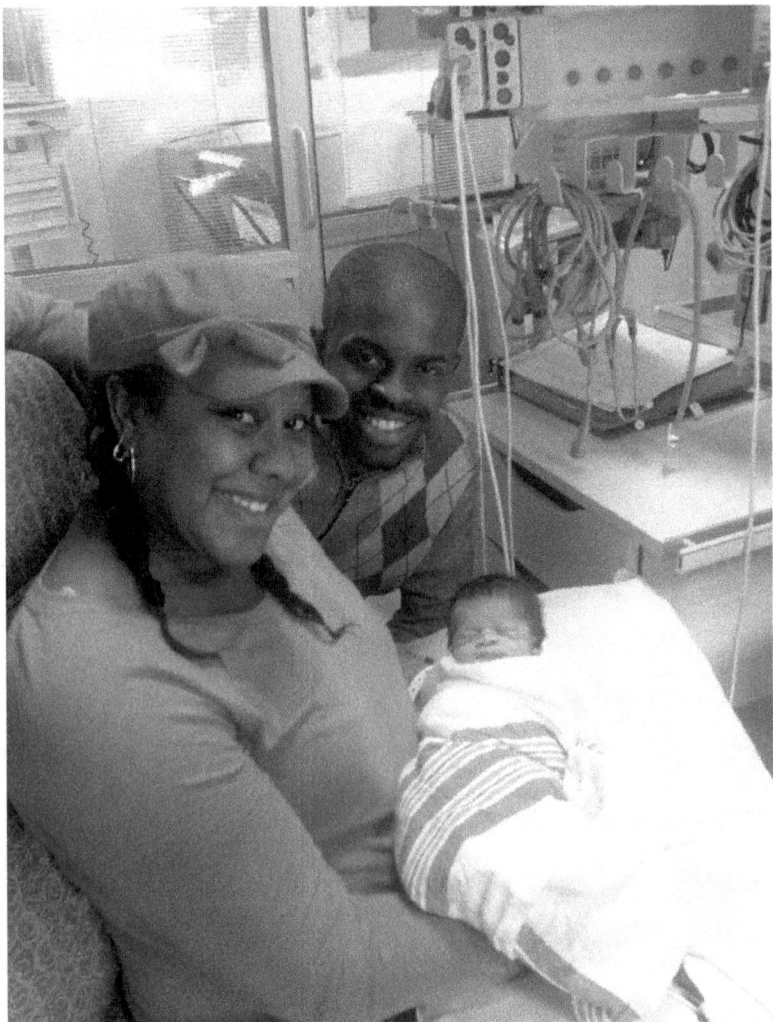

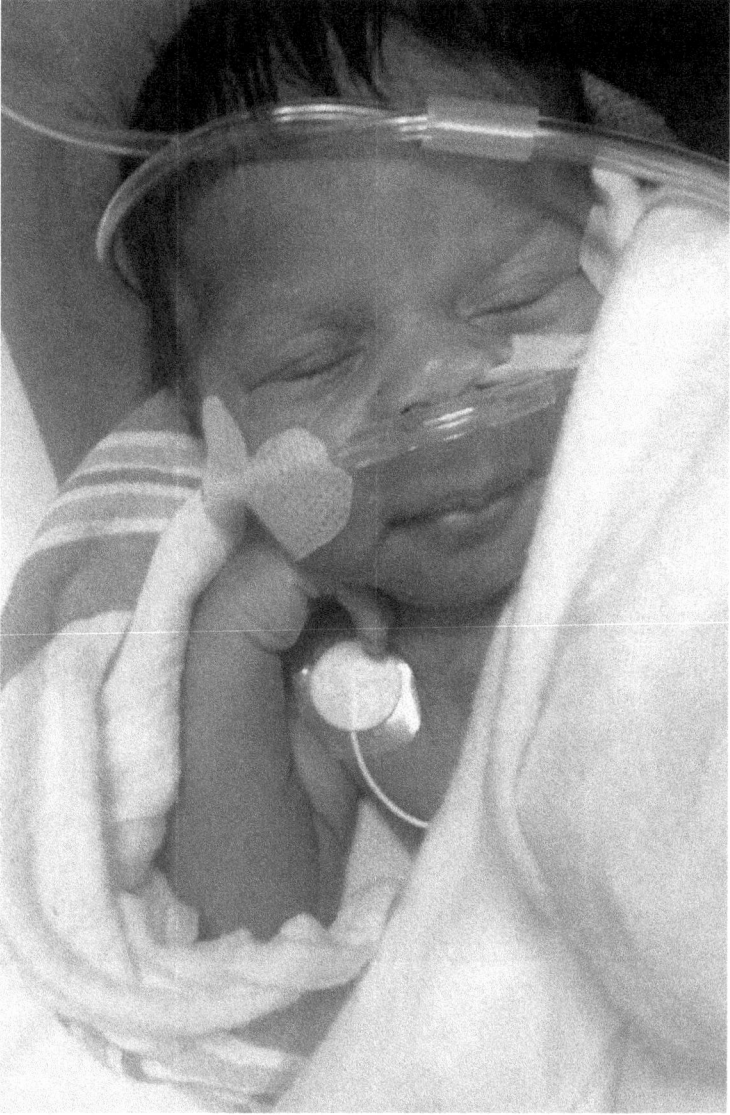

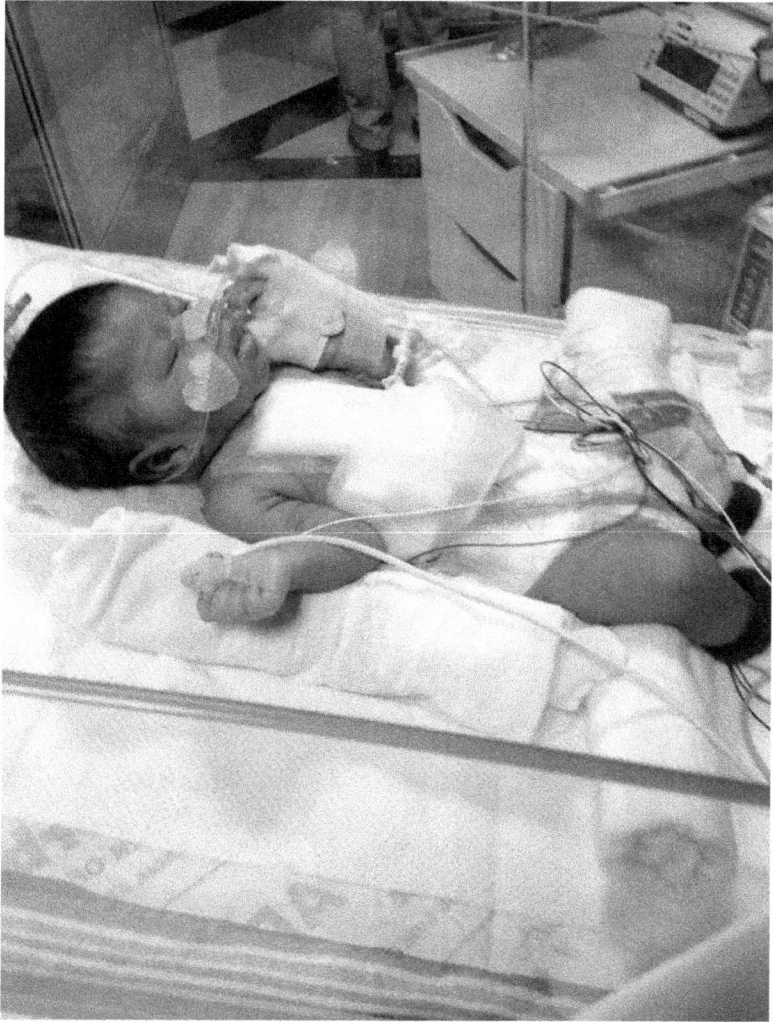

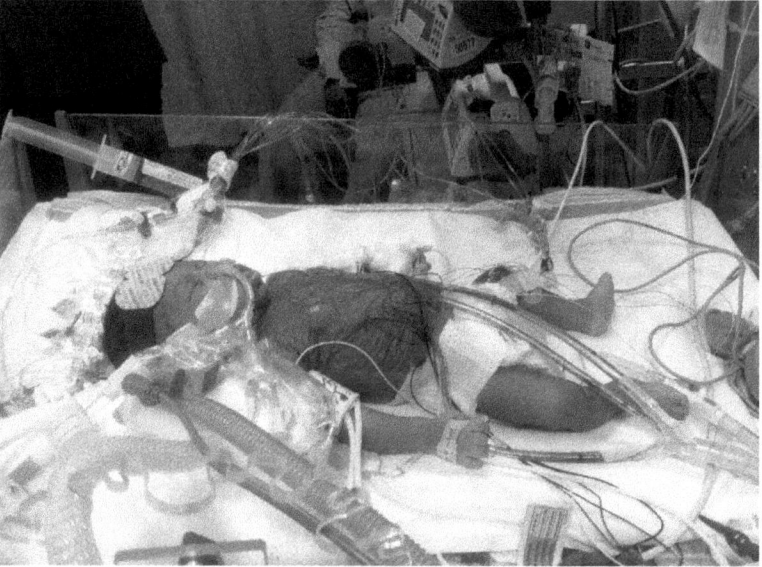

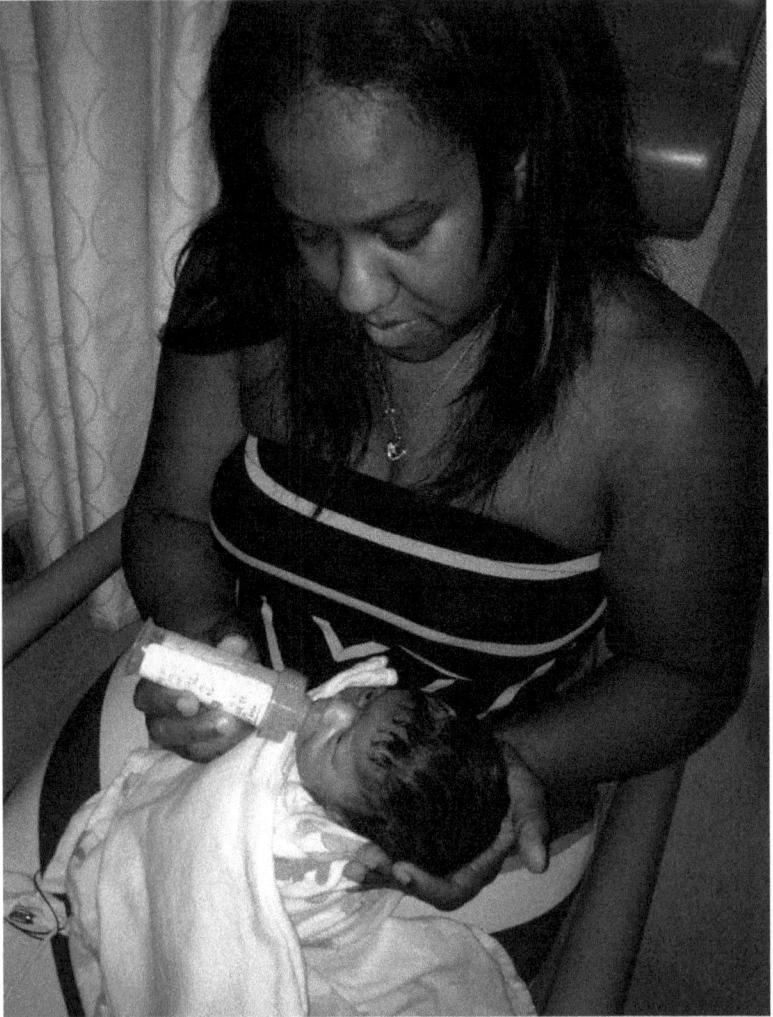

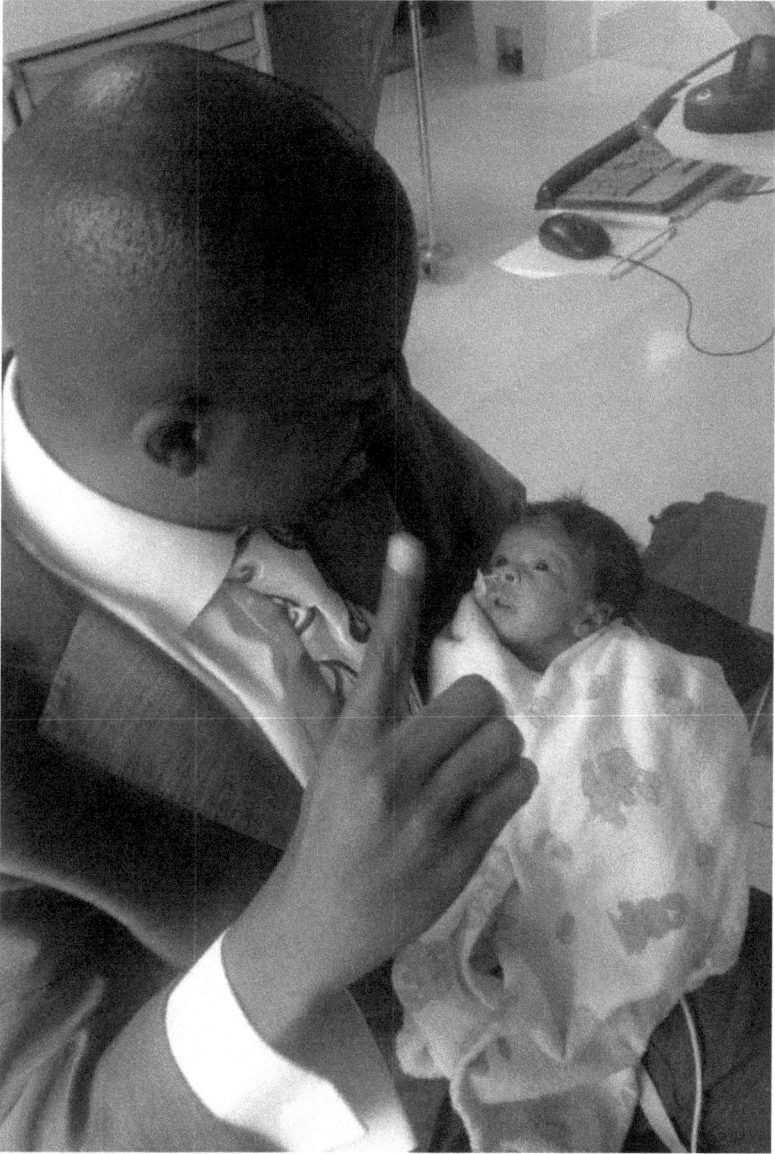

Charle' Johnson
January 18, 2014 · 👥

My Umbrella in the Storm ...Psalms 91:2 I will say of the Lord, He is my refuge and my fortress: My God; in him will I trust.

👍 108   2 Comments 1 Share

👍 Like   💬 Comment   ↗ Share

Charle' Johnson
January 20, 2014 · 👥

Today is Day #27. This baby is a survivor!! I know you guys are tired of #TeamEvan but i wont rest til this kid is home. #ThatsAll #EvansMom #SpeakLife #ClaimVictory....

👍 288   78 Comments 1 Share

👍 Like   💬 Comment   ↗ Share

Charle' Johnson
January 27, 2014 · 👥

Day #33...Woke up today & told myself this storm aint even about me. Thank you Lord for trusting me to show the city you are a miracle worker. Use me Lord...Have Your Way...Minister to your people...Show them your works through Evan's situation... #ItsNotAboutUs #TeamEvan #EvansMom

Charle' Johnson
January 29, 2014 · 👥

Day #35...🎵"I've" had some good days...I've had some hills to climb... I've had some weary days...And some sleepless nights...But when I look around...And I think things over...All of my good days...Outweigh my bad days
I won't complain!!!.....God's been so good to me...more than you or this ol world could ever be....🎵 #EvansMom

👍 165   24 Comments 1 Share

63

5 DAY

FORECAST

When looking at the 5-day forecast, you try to prepare for the weather for the week. In Southern California, where I reside, the weather is unpredictable. We never know what kind of weather we are going to have. The weather can change daily. We've even had 90-degree days in the wintertime. I have even seen some 80-degree days drop down to below fifty at night. I've also seen 100-degree days change to 60-degree days in 48 hours. That's how the months ahead in our life were. In other words, all over the place.

We were able to take advantage of the nursery we had prepared for him and use all our baby shower gifts. We put together the gadgets and gizmos we purchased with our gift cards. And most, we were finally able to sleep in our own bed. Rest was still hard to come by though because Evan woke up every three hours on time like a newborn. There were at least five medications I had to administer to him throughout the day. But our new normal was being created.

We couldn't quite get a grip on life. We were maintaining. The bills were all over the place. The money was there but I just couldn't keep up. My mind was on that baby being born and those surgeries and that hospital. I was doing the best that I could, to manage. But our main priority was focused on keeping Evan comfortable at home. We were settling in our newest addition to the family. We were getting acquainted with his personality. We never saw him laugh at the hospital. He only made plenty of facial expressions. When we heard him laugh for the first time, it was a warm feeling for both my husband and I. A weight was lifted from our shoulders as I remember us having the conversation about whether he was going to have a sense of humor or not.

My husband is a funny guy. I am 90% sure that if the Lord didn't call him to be a Pastor, he would be a Comedian and have a stand-up show on a DVD out right now. On the other hand, my sense of humor is sillier and goofier, and my husband is the one who cracks all the jokes and is witty with coming up with pranks. For example, my husband and our bonus son play pranks on each other all the time. I am always caught in the middle and must be a part of their plan. I must sit with a straight face as if I don't know what's going on. They like to play hide and seek and scare the living daylights out of each other.

For example, my husband once hid in his closet and waited for our bonus son to get out of the shower so he could jump out the closet to scare him. That took a lot of effort to stay in the closet that long just to scare a person to create laughter. We knew there had to be a funny bone somewhere in Evan's body. However, we thought seeing him in pain and being exhausted from all his surgeries, that maybe he would never smile at us. And then, one day it happened. He laughed at a toy and couldn't stop laughing for five minutes. My husband and I literally shed tears to see his first laugh come out. That was a moment we made sure to catch on video. We walked around with our camera's out to document every milestone. Especially since he was counted out. The baby who was going to have a life with minimal value, just laughed for the first time.

As Pastor and wife, we never missed a beat at the church either. Business was running as usual. I was slowly but surely making my way back to work. Evan still had quite a few doctors' appointments that we both went to. We had to make sure we both were fully aware of how to care for him and his incision, his diet, and of course his medications. I thought he had a specialist before, but he had way more now. He also had a nutritionist (for his poor weight gain), a geneticist (for his chromosome disorder), a cardiologist (for the heart of course), a nephrologist (for his kidney abnormality), a urologist (for his genitalia disorder), an electrophysiologist (for pacemaker following), and a good old fashion pediatrician (for all the regular baby stuff). But. of course, a pediatrician who dealt with high-risk cases.

He was still very fragile. We had to hold him a certain way because of his incision. He had to be bathed a certain way. And because he was small in weight there was a certain way, we had to mix his bottles. We began supplementing my breast milk with formula to help him gain some weight. It was a formula that we had to order online because most stores didn't carry it. I had to watch his breathing. There were certain signs and signals we had to be on guard for.

We had a few random moments where he was struggling to breath. They would call it reactive breathing. He would be in respiratory distress and break out into these sweats. It was hard to tell if it was from a cold, something he ate, or his heart. Your vigilance as a parent with a child with health challenges has to be on point. You have to know what to look for. You have to know when to move into action and when to stand down. Knowing when to call 911 or when you can take a chance and go to urgent care, are all moments that are driven by your gut. You have to do what you feel is best at that moment.

There were times I did both. I have called 911 and there were times where I felt it was safe enough for us to drive him to the ER ourselves. Most of the time it was him needing a breathing treatment or some suctioning to clear his airways. Because of his fragility, his immune system was prone to every virus and cold that came his way. We went from respiratory syncytial virus (RSV) to bronchial stress to pneumonia. There were a lot of small hospital visits and stays throughout the first six months of his life. Those ER visits were brutal. Because he had some small veins and scar tissue from early surgeries and lots of sticks already, it was always hard for them to get blood drawn. His veins would collapse on them every time.

This is where I learned how to advocate for my son. You really must know your rights as a parent. I had to be very stern with the ER med teams and let them know that he was a hard stick, and that they should bring someone into ER that worked with pediatrics and that isn't just an ER nurse. It's amazing how every time their response is, "We have one of the best phlebotomists in this department". And we say, ok we'll see. Then after watching Evan fuss, scream, squirm and holler, they end up bringing in someone from the pediatric department to draw his blood. My husband and I decided that every ER visit we would stand our ground and make them go get a pediatric nurse to draw his blood. We wouldn't put him through that trauma anymore.

We didn't entrust any babysitters. It was hard to leave him with anyone. He had so many instructions. It wasn't that we didn't trust anyone, it was more so because I didn't want to put that responsibility on a person to have to remember and know all the stuff my husband and I knew to administer and care for Evan. It was almost like he came with his own manual on how to care for him and hold him.

My brother was his first babysitter. We had to sit on a panel one night for a few hours, and we tested my brother out. We needed the fresh air. I typed up the medication list and made the bottles for him and my sister-in-love. They did good. And for a few hours we were able to breathe. There was light at the end of the tunnel. We knew we could go on a few more date nights.

We skipped date night and planned an impromptu 5-day trip to Rio, Brazil. After all we had been through, we were ready for a vacation. We gave my parents the honors of babysitting Evan for that trip. Since we had to be gone a little longer, we knew it may be a little easier and less stressful for all of us, if they kept Evan for those days. We skyped everyday just to check in. But we were able to let out some frustrations in the country and breathe in some South American air. We talked and laughed about what we had just come out of. We knew we had some more bridges to cross. They said one day he would need another heart surgery. They said one day he would need to have surgery on his genitals. None of us knew the date of "one day". We didn't live in fear or anticipation. We just took everything one day at a time.

TSUNAMI

Tsunamis and hurricanes are remarkably similar when it comes to damage. A tsunami is caused by a shift in the sediments of the ground undersea. They cause a large wave to come ashore and wipe out everything in sight. A tsunami can happen by itself or it can be caused by a hurricane. Storm surges caused by a hurricane can create a tsunami.

We received a call from the cardiologist days before our Brazil trip letting us know that Evan needed another heart surgery sooner rather than later because his arteries were beginning to close. The survival rate of babies after an arterial switch or correction is 98% but there is a small chance that after the switch, they can develop pulmonary stenosis, a narrowing in the arteries at the site of correction. What are the chances that Evan was a recipient of good old pulmonary stenosis? His arteries had narrowed, and they needed to go in and open them up. I didn't spend much time dwelling on it. I focused on my pending vacation and my husband and I agreed that we would face it when we returned.

Once we were back in the U.S., we set up the appointment for them to take a close look at his heart via a catheterization lab. That's where they put dye into your circulatory system and look at your heart and veins on a screen to see how your system is functioning. It's a same day procedure. They usually put you to sleep and then once you wake up and you can go home. We were able to wear our scrubs and walk with him into the procedure room and watch them administer the anesthesia. That was probably one of the most traumatizing things we've had to watch.

They placed the gas mask over his face as he's screaming, hollering and struggling to get away and then he was knocked out in about 10 to 30 seconds. After, we waited for the doctor's report. As usual, the doctor walked out before us being able to see Evan and told us his heart didn't look good and he would call us that week to schedule another surgery. It wasn't a shocker! We knew it was coming. I guess we just didn't think it was coming that soon.

Evan then went into recovery and we waited for him to fully recover so we could go home. This time, something was different when he came out of recovery. He looked miserable. He looked unhappy. He fussed at me, he fussed at my husband. He fussed at my mom, and he fussed at every nurse that came in to help. He couldn't keep anything down. The nurses thought he just needed more time for the anesthesia to wear off, but I knew something was wrong with him. After being in recovery for hours longer than expected the cardiologist came back in to see what was going on. As it turned out, that little procedure had sent him into congestive heart failure.

I was tired. I was weak. I was over it. We had just gotten home and were getting everything in order. I was back full time at work. Evan was eight months old, crawling and trying to talk. Everything was going so well. But a shift in his health caused a wave of unforeseen circumstances that then landed us in the hospital for forty-four days!

We were immediately transferred via ambulance from Kaiser Sunset to CHLA again, first to get him stable and then to prepare him for surgery that week. They had to make room on the schedule for him that week. His heart needed immediate attention. Neither me nor my husband had peace this time around. We were frustrated. We were angry. We wanted to fix it. But we didn't know exactly how or what we could do. We had to again sign the consent forms that included all of the usual risks and side effects at hand, like possible infection, damaged body parts that might be in the way during procedures, loss of blood and loss of life.

We didn't want to spend the night at the hospital neither did we want to eat the food. Word had started to get out that we were back at the hospital awaiting another open-heart surgery for our child. It seemed unreal. Had I not witnessed it myself, I would have thought it was a made-up story. Our network couldn't believe it either. Everyone was in shock as we began to update our Team Evan family.

My husband and I had both mentally checked out for a few days. And then Wednesday night came. It was time to prep Evan for surgery. We gave him his bath and watched a good movie with him until he knocked out. On the day of the surgery, we flooded the CT-ICU room this time. I think someone reported us. There were too many of us. But honestly, we didn't care. The anxiety and curiosity of Evan's situation became contagious. Everyone wanted to know what was going on with this little baby. He must be something special. The security guard would tell us we had a lot of calls to our room. We had to turn off calls to our room because it was too overwhelming. We had random people just showing up to the hospital to check on Evan and people were going to the hospital saying that they were family members, just to see Evan. It was mayhem, yet so rewarding to see this level of support.

Our social media timelines were full of Team Evan posts. People were tapping in across the city and the nation to pray for a little boy they had never seen. After 8 long hours, the surgeon came in with the report. He said it was one of the most complex cases of his career, but he did his best work and bought us more time. But unfortunately, Evan would need another surgery in the future. He just wasn't big enough for them to make the adjustments that they needed to make. Evan had pulmonary stenosis and double outlet right ventricle. To be honest, I don't even know what that means or the best way to explain it. All I know is, there is a narrowing of the arteries that keeps occurring. And it's hard to fix because there's an obstruction. Since Evan is so tiny, they are only able to fix it according to his current size, but once he outgrows that, they will need to do it again. I guess that's the mom version of what I gathered after all the doctor visits and consultations.

Recovery time was the same as the first surgery. They brought Evan back to his room with tubes everywhere. His chest was still slightly open to allow the swelling to go down. He was intubated like the first time. He had those large tubes on each side of his chest again for draining fluids. His personal nurse was running around the room again checking fluid levels, medication levels and more. By the evening he was off the breathing machine.

The next day they pulled out the chest draining tubes. But we noticed he was struggling to breathe. Respiratory therapist would come in to check and sure enough he was struggling to breathe. We found out that they had collapsed his diaphragm when they either placed the chest tube in his body or when they took it out. So, he had to go back into the operating room so that they could go in his side and pull down his diaphragm. This procedure is called a plication.

At this point, I was pretty upset and not directly at the hospital staff, just at the situation in general. I didn't know how much more my little baby would be able to take. He was already such a trooper the first time around, but I could see how he was frustrated and in pain this time. His little arm was all bandaged up and he would cover his face whenever the light would come on in his room. His hands were swollen from so many needle sticks and collapsed veins. His tiny fingers somehow still managed to grab his pacifier and put it in his mouth to soothe himself. His pacifier had been his best friend since he was two days old. I was totally anti-pacifier, but I guess they automatically give them to NICU babies to help them to learn to suck. It took us two years to ditch that thing. It was attached to him everywhere we went. It helped keep him calm and content.

After the plication, we sat waiting for his breathing to get back to normal. Things took a turn after that. I could sense the change in the atmosphere. My husband was tired and frustrated. As a dad, he wanted to be able to fix it. There was nothing we could do but wait it out and let his body recover. We allowed the hospital and staff to do their good work. Personally, I just wanted my baby back home, where he could be comfortable in his bed and playing with his own toys. Although, I did appreciate the toys, stuffed animals, and blankets we received as gifts from other moms whose children had passed away in the hospital. There were also the occasional celebrity visits passing out coffee and tea in the hallway in the mornings.

But I was tired of taking a shower in a shared parent shower in an ICU hallway. I had created the hashtag #FreeEvan on social media because I felt like my baby was in prison. Heck, I felt like I myself was in prison. We became aggravated with hospital staff as breathing treatments weren't working and he just couldn't catch his breath. After back and forth complaining, chest X-rays, and more tests ran, we finally figured out that there was a tear in his vocal cords from the breathing tube. The breathing tube being put inside his throat at such a small age so many times had damaged his throat and vocal cords. What did that mean? It meant that we were back to the operating room again for another round of anesthesia and him going under so that they could repair his throat.

We are now running on fumes at this point. Yet, I was steadfast. I was an open book listening to every doctor's report, making sure I followed what was going on and stayed on top of every medicine dose or treatment they gave him. I had no more tears left to cry and no emotions remained for me to show. I was like an empty shell just holding my baby, feeding my baby & doing whatever was necessary to help him thrive. Nothing and no one else in life mattered. This tsunami was all about saving Evan's life. Was he going to make it out of this?

Additionally, they had to change his diet. He could no longer swallow food or liquids like before. The little flap that closes off the windpipe when you eat is a part of what was damaged. So, every bottle of juice, milk, and water had to be thickened. It was another bullet point to add to the checklist for anyone babysitting him and also another cost. We did get his surgery bill after the first run of surgeries and hospital visits. Although we had insurance, the bill was now $80,000 in medical work and we didn't have that. I don't even know what happened to that invoice. But paying it was the last thing on my mind when it came in the mail.

Once his heart was stable, we were transported back to Kaiser. All we had to do was get his strength back and get his appetite back. It had been a long thirty-one days at Children's Hospital this time around. The week he was transferred back to Kaiser, we were moving but I was at the hospital every day, while my husband and his friends were packing up my house. When they moved him to Kaiser, I took a day away to go home refresh and pack the kitchen for the move. My brother and my sister-in-love went to check on Evan and sit with him that day. The next morning as I got up to get dressed and head to the hospital for updates, I received a call from a social worker who said that she hadn't seen any activity at the hospital and that we were neglecting him. We never left him alone. We always rotated. I told her I had been there every day and I needed a few hours to go home and gather myself and my house for the move. Her reply was that my child needed stimulation and he needed to see his parent's faces.

I wasn't very polite this time when I explained to her that this was my son's 31st day at the hospital, and that I have not neglected him once during this entire ordeal, since I was three months pregnant with him. She digressed as she said she was unaware that we had been in the hospital for thirty-one days. My next thought was *"Ma'am, make sure you check his chart, before you call with DPSS threats and talks of neglect because you don't know our story"*. This is EVAN!!! He has a whole network of support and I am far from an unfit mother!

As the days continued, we were now smack dab in the middle of our 5th Annual Pastor and Wife Anniversary. This Anniversary service is one of our biggest celebrations of the year. We get all dressed up to celebrate with our members and our other Pastor friends. It is a time of reflection and giving. A time where we shed good tears about how far we have come and then prepare for the future.

We left the hospital, went home and got dressed. Upon entering the celebration, neither of us could hold back the tears or enjoy the moment because we were missing our son. We were worried about our son. That week he would not eat any food by mouth. He had a tube in his nose for his milk. He was declining instead of progressing. They wanted to put a GI tube in his stomach so that he could get his necessary nutrients and calories. They were really concerned about his low weight and lack of interest in eating. They had asked me to sign off on the consent for the procedure and I declined. I didn't want him to have a GI tube. I didn't think he needed it and I didn't want another foreign object inside of his tiny body.

And I for sure wasn't going back to the operating room. Enough was enough!

Years later looking back at it, I was probably being selfish because I was tired. But the truth is, in that moment, I really was being an advocate for my son who did not have a voice for himself. In my gut, I did not think he needed it. I knew he was miserable and wanted to be at home. It was about a week of back-and-forth conversations with doctors and being told by doctors that they were going to report me to Children's Services for going against what they thought was medically best for my child.

At that point, even my husband and my parents said maybe I should consider the procedure. I told all of them *"No!"* I knew what the Lord told me in my spirit. So, that night when we entered the celebration we were overwhelmed with various emotions. I guess the Pastors and guests could see it on our faces because they interrupted the celebration to literally pray heaven down on our behalf. That's what friends do. They step in the trenches of your storms with you. They bring umbrellas, food, laughter and good cheer, even when you don't ask them to.

That night when I said thank you to family, friends, and our church members, I made sure to also brief them on Evan's current condition. Something rose up in my spirit that night where I proclaimed that no matter what the doctors had said and even though it looked like he wasn't going to bounce back this time around, there was a "BUT GOD" in my spirit! I was weak and tired in my body, then I was quickly reminded of Psalms 34:1 *"Many are the afflictions of the righteous but [God] delivers him out of them all".*

They knew I had one more day to decide about that GI Tube procedure. And I stood flat-footed on that stage that night and declared that my child would not need that GI Tube because I believe what God told me in my spirit. The Lord's voice is always louder than the wind in your storm.

We were moving that week and my mom had taken a few days off to help me between hospital visits and the house, since my husband would be tied up with moving. My mother and I went to the hospital and the doctors had another meeting with us. They asked me to take home and watch the DVD on how to care for a child with a GI tube. They wanted me to know what the recovery would look like after the procedure. I told them they could keep the DVD because I wasn't going home to watch it. They asked me to sign the consent, and I refused again. They told me that Children's services were going to get involved and I should be prepared to receive a call from them and that I should rethink my decision. I honestly did not care about any of that.

That night, I was prepared for the worst on the next day. I knew I had to unpack boxes and my mom would be at the hospital with Evan. I knew that I would get a call from her with bad news or that Children's services had come by, BUT GOD... I was in the middle of unpacking in Evan's new room and hanging up his clothes. My mom called and said, "Get up here and bring the car seat." I thought she was joking. Evan's cardiologist said to give Evan a chance to go home and get comfortable. He said that his colleagues wouldn't agree with him, but that he was making an executive decision. Even adults don't bounce back from the types of surgeries and procedures that Evan has had back-to-back so why would they expect that from an eight-month-old baby. The one stipulation was that I had to give a daily report to the cardiologist on what Evan ate for the day, and if he didn't eat at home like he was supposed to, then I had to bring him back and readmit him.

Of course, I agreed to that with no hesitation. I grabbed my shoes, I grabbed Evan's car seat and I was on the freeway to get my child before they changed their mind. It was also my dad's birthday the same day. We didn't tell my dad the good news. I just invited him over to see our new home. His birthday gift that year was a big hug and a smile from his firstborn grandson in the comfort of my home.

Over the next couple of days Evan regained his appetite. And just like that, we were back to enjoying his presence at home. After 44 long days, just one week longer than the first hospital run. I didn't want to see another hospital, or doctor, or nurse. I was traumatized. I had questions. I was a damaged first-time mom. The storm had wiped me out. I lost my identity. I went from being Charlé to Evan's Mom. I was Evan's caregiver. I was Evan's advocate. I was Evan's protector. I had a responsibility, and nothing was more important than helping him thrive.

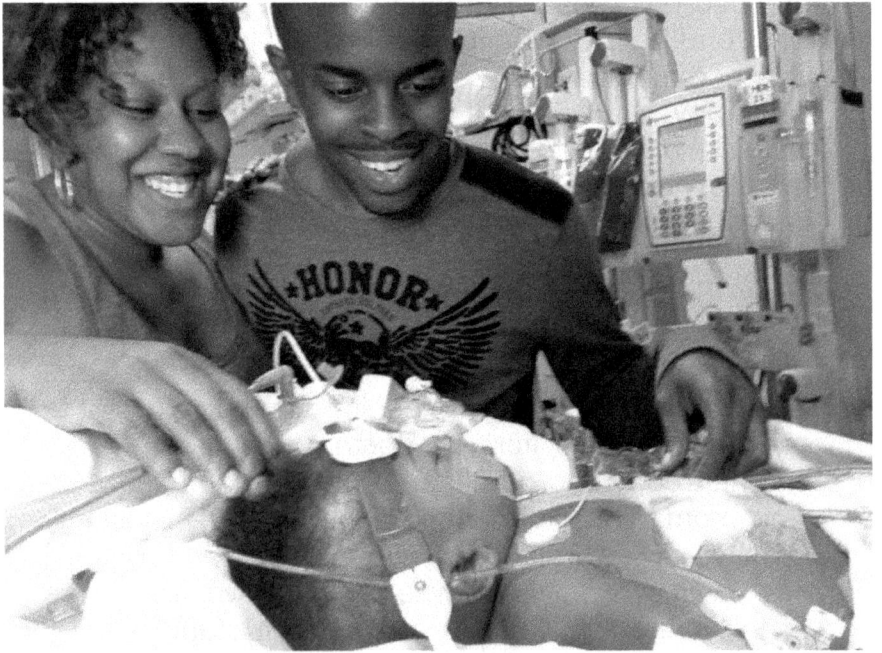

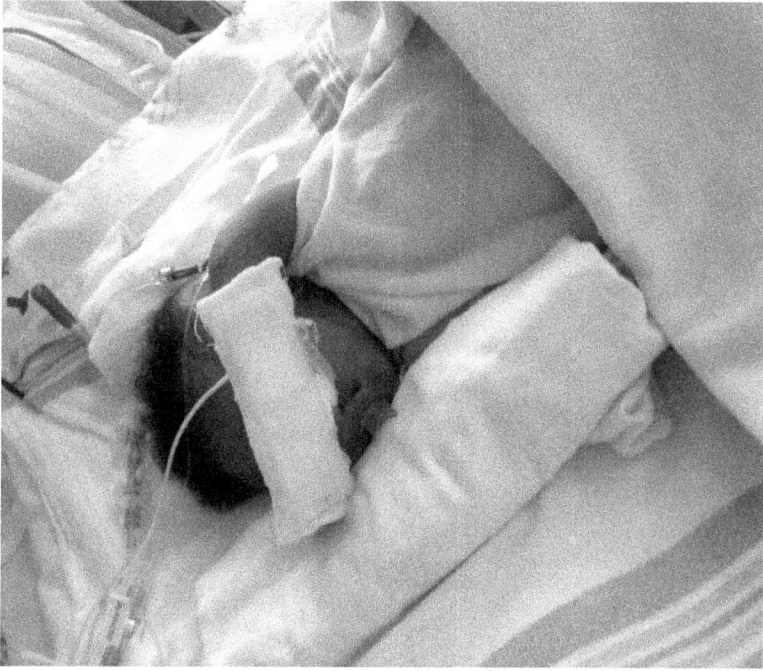

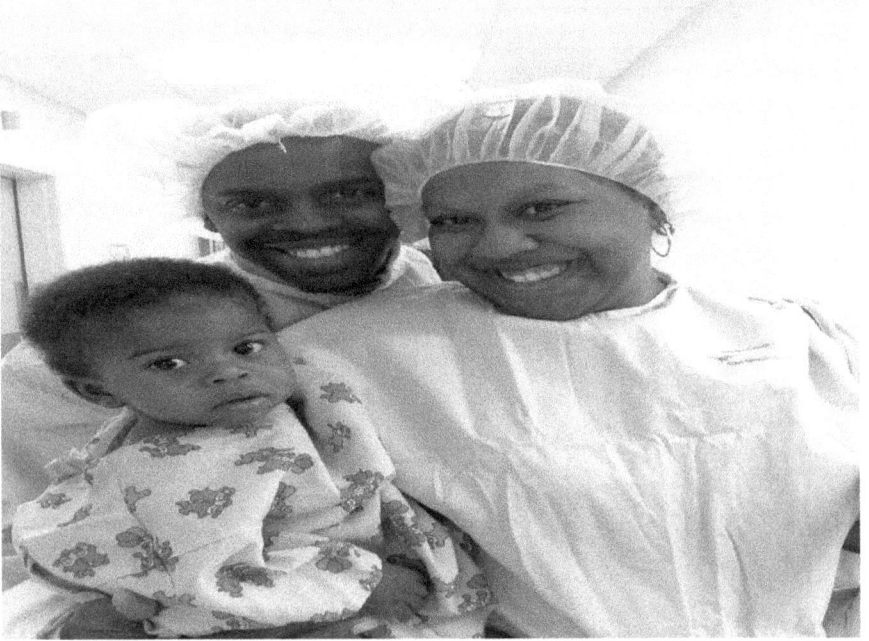

GLOOMY

When I think about gloomy weather, I immediately see a dark or depressing type of day. It's usually a day that is low in spirits with heavy clouds and feelings of melancholy. Gloomy days pass but they can also linger.

Evan finally came home in October after that long stay. I was so discombobulated that although he was home, I just couldn't get my emotions together to get happy. I felt like there was just so much to do like doctor's appointments, medications, watch his diet, thicken cups of juice, water and milk, watch his breathing at night while he slept, and so on. As well as the underlying fear of when was the next open-heart surgery.

We were still playing what felt like round robin with all of his appointments and specialist. After getting Evan settled back in at home, my husband had a lump on his neck the size of a lemon that seemed to grow out of nowhere. It was like we kept getting hit back-to-back with the health challenges. I couldn't process if we were under attack or if this was orchestrated by God. But it was too much.

Evan was not well enough to be at daycare. His chest cavity was still tender from all the surgeries, so he had to be carried a certain way. I had exhausted my paid family leave, so technically I was supposed to be back at work. Thank God for longevity because they didn't fire me and were understanding about my situation. We were still getting used to thickening his liquids and increasing his appetite. I needed a break or breather but never saw one in sight.

As his first birthday approached, I thought of the perfect theme. What more could we do for a Christmas baby other than turn his birthday party into The North Pole? It was the most exciting thing we saw that entire year! We had fake snow on the ground, a hot cocoa station, an arts and crafts station. The church staff was dressed as reindeers and elves and The North Pole isn't complete without a visit from Santa.

After the New Year, I was back at work and trying to do ministry again. I helped my husband as much as I could. I also had a praise dance group that traveled and ministered across the city, attending conferences. But my mind was hitting and missing. I was showing up 50% at work and church. I could no longer complete tasks because I wasn't focused.

My husband had surgery on his neck a month after Evan came home. I somehow managed to be there to care for him and Evan, during recovery. I did it all out of love, but must admit that at some point, I was growing weary. I was trapped in the house, nursing everyone else back to health, while I myself was fading away. I wondered if I was upholding the standard of being a strong mom and a caring wife? I wanted to make my village proud, but I was not ok. I was crying on the inside even as Evan was recovering and doing well day to day.

I felt like postpartum had kicked in a year later for me. Everything I went through in the last year and a half had come crashing down. I was flat out tired and stressed just thinking about the storm I had endured. Was my adrenaline flowing so much that I didn't pay attention to the hurt and trauma it was causing me? I was bred to tough everything out and never let the world see you sweat. My endurance had peaked, and it was over.

When Evan was healthy enough and only needed medication in the morning and at night, I finally trusted that he could go to daycare. I would still mix his bottles and liquid to make sure it was the right amount of thickness for his throat. He went part time so I could try and go back to work and so that Evan can be in environments with other children and people. He needed a change of scenery from the hospital and the house as well.

I attempted to go back to work, but I was still forgetting everything. I started falling asleep at the wheel from being so exhausted. My husband would talk with me all the way home or all the way to work. It's interesting when you are trying to pull yourself out of an emotional shut down. I didn't know what to call my symptoms and I was trying to self-diagnose. I was too prideful to share with any family members or a therapist how I was really feeling on the inside. I knew something was wrong when I would be in emotional settings and I couldn't drop one tear. It's like I had psyched myself out. I made myself believe that I was so strong and tough that I wasn't in touch with my real feelings. I couldn't find them.

What made it worse is that I wasn't sure who noticed. No one ever really asked, not because they didn't care, but probably because I always said I was good.

My favorite line is *"I'm good and even when I ain't good, I'm good."* I had perfected smiling through the pain. Everyone always asked about Evan and I would give the full run down on his status and recovery and I felt like there wasn't any room left to talk about how I was feeling or how tired I was. Additionally, what was I going to do about being tired? I couldn't change my situation.

I could tell my husband was in the same season. People still had demands, expectations, and requests from us and seemingly forgetting all that we had endured. But we made ourselves available because we are servants. We never gave up on God or His people. We were walking billboards for hope and faith, but we had become so empty on the inside.

It's dangerous when both spouses are in depression together. We were taking turns with good days and bad days. It wasn't healthy for either one of us. But we had no choice but to stick it out. I believe this was one of those moments where being equally yoked, matters. I'm grateful that we both knew how to tap into the Spirit. Although we were both at low points, I know he was praying for me and I was praying for him.

Some days my husband would lie in the bed with all of the blinds closed and the cover over his head. I wouldn't nag or bother him. I would go about my day and pray for him, so much as to weep for him. I know that as the head of our family, and a Pastor at that, seeing us go through that storm hurt him. Men like to fix things and there was nothing he could do to fix Evan's heart or my heartache as a mother.

We were home and Evan was thriving, but in our hearts, we knew we were not out of the woods. We still had a responsibility to help Evan thrive. Evan had physical therapy appointments because he had weak leg muscles due to lying in the hospital with no leg stimulation during his developmental stages. He couldn't lift his leg high enough to climb steps or to straddle the toys that most toddlers love to ride. They would hook him up to the smallest treadmill to build his leg strength. The therapist also gave us some exercises to do with him at home. We had to process that this is our new normal and that now we have a child who has serious health challenges, and our world will always revolve around Evan and that fact. This was a dark time for us. We spent a lot of time at home just focusing on us, rebuilding each other and watching Evan learn to walk and talk. We were low in spirit, but we were together.

SONSHINE

Sometimes the sun comes out after a storm. I've even seen sunshine on a rainy day. There's a folklore that says if the Sun is out while it's raining then the devil is beating his wife. I'd like to think that it's God's way of saying although you're in a storm, I am still with you.

By now, my husband started to crack jokes about having another child or that Evan needed a playmate. I would laugh it off. But deep down I was like no, absolutely not. After the anxiety and emotional stress of carrying my first born, I noticed that even thinking about another baby gave me all kinds of added anxiety and pressure. What if it happened again? What if the reason for the birth defects weren't random but were because of me? I couldn't handle carrying another seed and was worried. Doubt and fear would interrupt the excitement of expecting. Not to mention, I thought it was very selfish to bring another child into the mix while Evan was getting so much attention. He was still so delicate and required so much. Would I be able to manage another human while Evan still had plenty of doctors' visits & his health challenges craved my presence?

My husband thought it would be a great idea to take a vacation to Miami to escape all that we had endured and to take a breather. After all, we had another heart surgery scheduled for some time that year. I am pretty sure his plans were to get me pregnant in Miami. But to our surprise again, we already had another passenger on board.

While touring the celebrity yachts in Miami, I had a strange feeling. Once you've carried one child, you learn different things about your body. When I ordered M&M peanuts and some cheddar pringles that day, I thought the combination of Pringles & M&M's never tasted so good. So as the tour guide said Usher and P Diddy's yacht is to the left, I leaned over to my husband and said we must visit the gift shop when we return to the hotel. I didn't really need the pregnancy test. I already knew I was pregnant because my body told me. After taking the test and seeing the pink line pop up, I immediately fell to my knees in tears in our hotel room. I broke down like a baby. I remember hyperventilating and telling my husband how I couldn't do it. I remember asking God to help me. I just held my husband's hand tight and began crying out to God. I asked for strength, peace, and calm in the storm.

This second pregnancy was nothing but cool breeze and smooth sailing the entire time. There were no complications. I still harbored a level of anxiety because of my previous situation. I wanted to have high hopes. And there was plenty to celebrate. He was due two days after my birthday, which meant another Capricorn, another winter baby, and that we made a baby almost the same time within two years.

In my heart, I really wanted the second pregnancy to be a girl so that we could be done with expanding our family. I could not take the emotional anxiety that surrounded pregnancy after the trauma of the first one. Not to mention, my mom had two children, so I knew I could manage two. I wasn't too certain about how stair step kids worked, but it looked good and easy when I saw other families walking through the mall or the grocery store.

When we went to find out the gender of our baby, I was convinced that we were having a girl. My mind told me it was a girl, or I tricked myself into believing it was a girl because I wanted to be done with pregnancies. My husband recorded on his phone as the doctor pulled up the ultrasound. First thing I noticed was, there was a huge difference between this ultrasound and our first born. We could see all of the organs and body parts on the screen. It was then when I understood how they knew things were going wrong with the first one.

We had the same doctor for the second pregnancy. And although she only dealt with babies with anomalies or special cases, she insisted on taking us in. I was so grateful. She made us comfortable because she knew our story and our history. She shed tears with us as she worried about whether Evan was going to make it or not. She was so excited to hear how he was thriving outside of the belly. She walked us through the entire process of the second pregnancy and was able to compare the difference in the findings. I almost slid off the table when she yelled with excitement that it was another baby boy! My frustration only lasted a few seconds and then I joined in with the celebration.

I was three months pregnant with our second child, when Evan's doctor called and said they were ready to review the dates for Evan's next surgery. They picked a date where we were supposed to be in New

Orleans for a huge Full Gospel Fellowship Conference. We had to cancel our trip at the last minute. Although we were looking forward to being poured into, the praise and worship, the late-night services, and good food and music from the French Quarter, Evan's health was our top priority.

We were prepped as usual, consent forms signed, bath the night before, etc. The only difference is that this was the first time where we were at home prior to the surgery and had to drive him to the hospital first thing in the morning. We were able to pack a bag for all of us to prepare to stay for however long the recovery lasted. He had his best friend, his pacifier with him, his favorite Paw Patrol blanket, a few of his favorite toys, and he was talking a little bit now at one and a half years old. He still wasn't fully aware of what was happening, but he had sense enough to know what the hospital looked like, and when he wanted to be held versus sitting in the hospital crib.

We filled the waiting room as usual with ten to fifteen family members, full of laughs, jokes and stories to keep our minds occupied and off the waiting game. Since I was pregnant this time around, it was a little harder for me to get comfortable. But I had a pillow and a blanket to help as much as possible.

Our Team Evan family was following and checking in on social media. This procedure wasn't as long as the others lasting maybe about four to five hours. But it never gets easier. My stomach gets in knots every time as I pray that they can fix what they need to fix and that my baby can come out of surgery, wake up and be off the breathing machine. And this time, my husband and I were able to tell the doctors to be careful when placing that breathing tube in his throat. We couldn't afford any repeats or unnecessary setbacks this time around.

Since he was older and bigger, they were able to do more. And he was more resilient this time around. I noticed that the hardest part about the recovery this time around, was that he wanted to sit in my lap all the time. I think Evan knew I was pregnant. He wanted to be up under me the whole time. I was uncomfortable in the chair. But I toughed it out to make sure Evan was good and content.

For the first surgery, the nurses had taught us how to hold a pillow in our laps, almost like the baby boppy to keep him comfortable and our arms comfortable while we held him. Same machines, same medication and fluid lines were running everywhere. The same irritating beeps and alarms made noises throughout the night and the same CT-ICU staff came in every three hours to check for vitals and every six hours for respiratory therapy. My husband had become a pro at suctioning the fluid out of Evan's nose and mouth. Because of the way Evan was laying, the secretions would build up in his throat and he would choke. The nurses had taught him how to use the machine, so we didn't have to wait on them to do it if they were busy doing other things. We toughed it out for 10 long days and then we were going home.

The surgery was not as bad as the first three surgeries; I think we could see a little bit of sun peeking through the clouds. The recovery was not as bad either, but enough to remember how much my back hurt because I couldn't move around like I wanted to from comforting my baby in my arms and baking the one in my belly. Yes, the major difference here was that I was pregnant with our second baby during this recovery period for Evan.

Imagine after everything I went through to then having a perfect pregnancy. And by perfect, I mean no extra specialist, no extra appointments, no weekly test, no unnecessary pokes. Then boom, a week passed the due date and still no baby. God has a sense of humor. The first baby was predicted to have a complicated delivery but came through like a champ. The second baby was predicted to have a great pregnancy and simple delivery. And yes, everything was good with my second pregnancy, until this baby just would not come down. The most stubborn of all my babies, showed us his identity in the womb. He just would not come down.

The umbilical cord was wrapped around the baby. They had already broken my water, so they had to put water back in my amniotic sac to cushion him during contractions. Just imagine a water hose inserted inside of you, while your dad is still in the room beside you. Then, five doctors come running in because my alarms are going off on monitors. We have already seen the scattering of doctors before, so we knew something was up. Tears fell from my face as I began to cry out to the Lord once again. *"Lord, Why me?" What is it about my babies that keeps bringing this adversity and these challenges?* My husband was in tears and my parents were in tears. I remember my dad saying he was tired of watching me go through this. The residue of Evan's trauma rested on all of us.

After an emergency C-section, our baby boy number two, Elijah Blake was born. Although the delivery scared us for a brief forty five minutes, him being born was the sunshine and the *sonshine* we needed in the middle of the storm. I was worried about him living in Evan's shadow. Evan requires so much attention, so many instructions, and so many hospital visits. Evan has his own Facebook page. He has his own following. When people see us in the mall, they recognize him before they recognize us, his parents. Despite all of that, Elijah made sure we remembered his arrival. His personality fills a room. He makes sure you remember him when you leave his presence. It was refreshing to see that he has his own personality and has his own identity already.

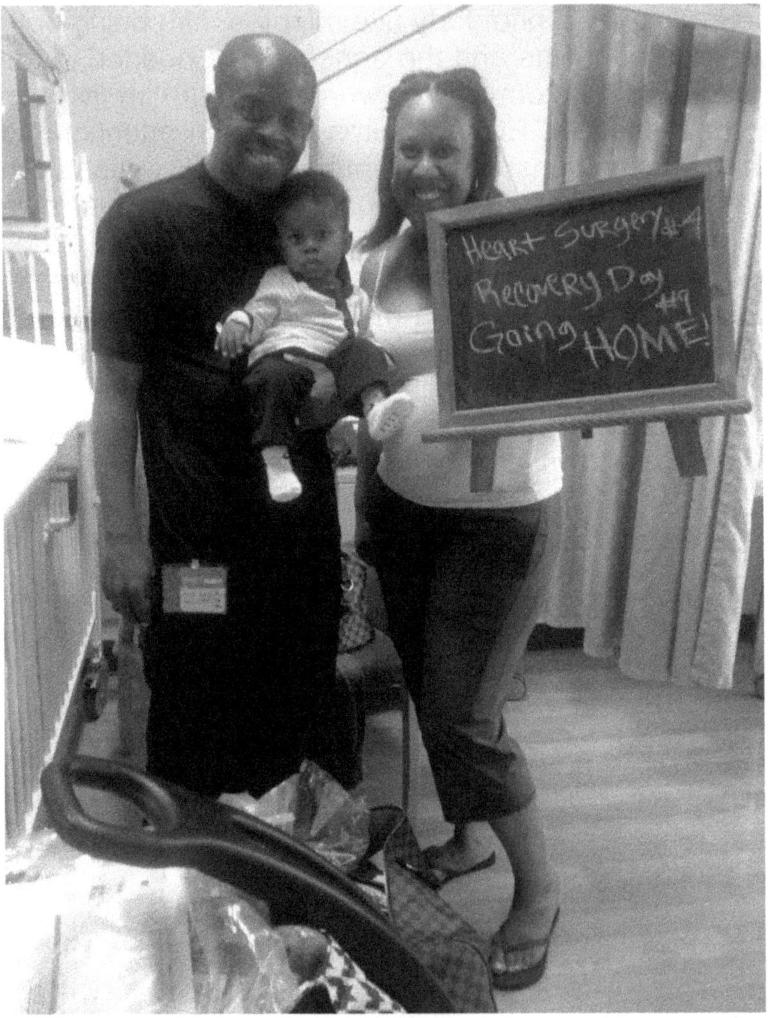
Heart Surgery #4
Recovery Day #9
Going HOME!

PINK SKIES

If you happen to look up and see a pink sky, it can mean quite a few things. According to Scientists, pink skies at night means that there will be good weather the next day. If there are pink skies in the morning, it means there will be bad weather the next day. Spiritually, when you see a pink sky, it represents love and peace. I'd like to think that in this season, a pink sky of love and peace hovers over the Johnson home.

We now have a house of six which includes our adult son, Trenton, 20 years old, Evan who is 7 years old, Elijah currently 5 years old and our baby girl, Charlee who is 1 ½. The Lord saw the desires of our hearts and blessed us with her after our storms ceased. Charlee has brought such peace to our lives and caused us to slow down.

I never saw myself being a mother of three (and counting my bonus son, a mother of four). We prepped for the first and third child but Elijah, our second child snuck up on us. They all add a different flavor to the house. The best way to manage is to come to grips with the fact that our reality will include chaos every now and then. We've cried so many days that we try our hardest to laugh as often as we can.

Secondly, we had to understand that our norm is different from the next family's norm and we cannot compare our house to someone else's. Then we had to create the best norm for our household. We aren't on a schedule, but we have a system that works for us (on most days). We create memories and enjoy all their personalities and it's important to stay connected to God for strength.

Having a house full of active boys keeps me on my toes. Wrestling and boxing matches can get a little intense. The occasional ninja or power ranger stunts can run me low. And Evan has now joined Daddy and big brother in their prank wars. At least, I don't have to remind them that Evan has a pacemaker anymore. They tell each other now and from time to time I'll hear in the background *"Don't tackle him like that; his pacemaker is right there."* or when Elijah gets really mad, he'll playfully threaten and yell *"Evan leave me alone or I will kick you in your pacemaker"* Of course, Elijah would never really do that. He is the typical little brother and although he threatens in the moment, he does not allow anyone else to do it or get close to his brother's pacemaker. I've overheard Elijah tell adults and other children alike to back away from his brother and not to hurt him.

We have also mastered making certain that Evan isn't anywhere in the kitchen when we start the microwave. And we enjoy going to the airport because of his pacemaker, we no longer must wait in long lines at TSA security or at amusement parks. The challenge is more so explaining to the school's nurse or staff about Evan's condition. I try to approach it gently, so they leave room to play and have fun. But I also will become stern enough, so they understand the severity of the situation. I don't want Evan to live in a bubble. My desire is for him to enjoy life being a boy.

We have a green light constantly flashing in our bedroom on our dresser that connects remotely from Evan's pacemaker to his doctor's cell phone. They can see when something is wrong, or something is happening with his pacemaker. That was a big boy upgrade in 2018. The original pacemaker they installed had a battery life of three to five years. It was a small one because Evan was so small at the time of installation.

For the first three years we visited the pacemaker clinic, they would call us on the cordless phone contraption and have us connect Evan to the machine. These are reasons why my husband and I feel like you might as well call us doctors. We have seen all kinds of devices during this journey. Even with all of the checkups and devices, Evan still isn't able to play contact sports. He loves sports though. He is my favorite football and basketball commentator. He can tell you play by play what is going on in the game. Evan loves to play the drums as well. He will stack up pots, pans, toys, shoe boxes, or anything to create a drum set. He uses pens and pencils, spoons and straws for sticks. He does have a few drum sets, but he enjoys creating his own.

We are all a part of Evan's efforts to thrive. After seven years, we've learned how to play our roles to protect him but also allow him to live life to his fullest potential. Evan no longer needs medication for his heart. Sure, we may have a few emergency room visits here and there, and he has to get all his dental treatments at CHLA because of his heart history. We may have a few scares with falls and anxiety about when is his next open heart surgery or our next long hospital stay, but we have found our rhythm.

We celebrate life every day because every day we wake up is a blessing. Every day that Evan wakes up is a blessing. We pray as a family as often as we can. Evan likes to lead our family prayer time, so we let him kick it off. Every year when Christmas comes around, we remind Evan how blessed he is and how he survived the odds set before him. We donate toys and books to Children's Hospital in Los Angeles. When we left the hospital in January 2014, after his first round of surgeries, we came home with bags of toys, stuffed animals, and blankets, donated by moms and families who had endured similar struggles. I knew we would do the same.

Evan asks a lot of questions about his health now. He knows his wounds are scars from surgery. He doesn't remember any of the early ones. We've shown him pictures and he'll ask to see them on his own. He still gets frantic by blood being drawn, shots or needles. Personally, I dread every ER or visit to the dentist. On these occasions, Evan will scream and holler and by this everyone in the waiting room will know that he is in the building. Some days I care enough to let them know that he has endured trauma at an early age, and other times, I just keep pushing holding back the tears and then cry my eyes out in the car.

I am proud of myself. I am proud of my family. We have fought a good fight together. Out of all our children, Evan requires a lot of love and attention. We believe that he has a level of separation anxiety because of all of the hospital visits. We have always been there with him. He doesn't know what life is like without mommy and daddy by his side. He doesn't like when the family is separated in the house. If Evan can have his way, we would all be in the same room watching the same movie or engaging in the same activity all day, every day.

As he is growing up, I can tell that we now must focus on his emotional wellbeing, rather than him thriving physically. Now that he is old enough for us to have conversations about his early years, and how he has to be vigilant about his health away from the family, he now understands how to sit down when he is running around too much. He knows that he is different from his siblings.

One day, Evan crawled up in a ball on our bed and asked us why he was sick and why was this happening to him? My husband and I both shed a tear with Evan. In that moment, we let him know that he is perfect and our little miracle. We reminded him that he is our warrior and capable of surviving anything.

THE SURVIVAL.

One of my favorite bible stories is that of Paul and the crew of prisoners on a ship during a storm. Paul warned the captain about the disaster ahead. The storm was too much for their lives and the ship. However, they didn't listen to Paul, and continued to set sail. In the middle of the storm God visits Paul at night and tells him that there will be no loss of life, only the ship. Acts 27:23-26 (msg) *"Last night God's angel stood at my side, an angel of this God I serve, saying to me, 'don't give up, Paul. you're going to stand before Caesar yet—and everyone sailing with you is also going to make it.' So, dear friends, take heart. I believe God will do exactly what he told me. But we're going to shipwreck on some island or other."*

He knew that there was a storm ahead and that their travels would be rough, but he believed the report of the Lord. Before they hit shore, the soldiers jumped ship. The ship was so damaged the only way they could make it to bay was by swimming. Even during the swimming for their lives, the soldiers still set out to attack Paul and the prisoners and the centurion was determined to save Paul and stopped them. They all abandoned the damaged ship and swam to shore for safety. Acts 27:44 (kjv) *"and the rest, some on boards, and some on broken pieces of the ship. And so, it came to pass, that they escaped all safe to land."*

Google defines survival as the state or fact of continuing to live or exist, typically despite an accident or ordeal, and difficult circumstances. For Paul and his crew, they survived the storm, shipwreck, and attempted attacks from the soldiers. Although the ship was busted up and damaged, they didn't lose their lives. They swam ashore on broken boards and pieces with plenty of bruises I'm sure, but the promise of God still prevailed. For the Johnsons we survived our personal storm of our son being born and enduring those five open heart surgeries and countless procedures thus far. He may have some bruises and scars, but he didn't lose his life. We may be emotionally scarred and bruised up, but we didn't lose our lives. and the promises of God have prevailed. We are still surviving. We are in this thing for all of Evan's life. This journey is ongoing. When we become too laxed is when we are hit with surprises.

During one of the largest pandemics in U.S. history, COVID-19, we had to take Evan to the ER because he had chest pains. He kept grabbing his chest saying, *"Mommy my heart hurts"*. I kept thinking; we are not going to ER in the middle of this global pandemic. He had been fine for years and then all of a sudden having chest pains.

While sitting in the ER, I thought about the number of mommies and families that we've encouraged along the way and how it has brought so much joy to my heart. When they call me and say their child has been diagnosed with medical challenges or that their baby will have birth defects and what should they do? Can I pray with them? Why this cross? Why this pain? How do you survive? I tell them the truth.

There have been several days where I was completely worn out and would just have random breakdowns. But I never allowed my children to see me cry. This life is nonstop caring for Evan. He needs so much attention emotionally and physically. The day he uttered the words that I am allowing the doctors to hurt him, it crushed me to the core. It was the first time that I almost felt guilty. I never wanted to watch him suffer or live a life where he thought I would let anyone constantly hurt him.

On one of my personal "bad" days, I drove into the city for cheer practice. I had become a high school Cheer Coach after switching to an Independent Contractor. We needed more income, plus it was my high school and I had cheer experience and a love for the school. As I was walking on campus to my classroom, I felt the gulp in my throat. I was about to have a breakdown right then and there. I couldn't contain it. Of course, I didn't want the cheer squad to see me. I walked into the office and thank God the principal was there. I completely broke down in her office. It was just the two of us.

Later, I found it interesting that she wasn't supposed to be in her office that day. It was during the summertime, when most of the faculty isn't present, and the principal just happened to be there handling some business. Her and I were able to talk mom to mom, and although she doesn't have a child with health challenges, she was able to minister to me that day woman to woman. You never know how God can use you.

That day wasn't about being a mom; it was about not allowing myself to operate on empty and remembering to put on my oxygen mask first so that I can help everyone else. The lesson here is, you can't survive if you never come up for air. You cannot let your circumstance drown you. Self-care is key, even though there are so many moments where I feel self-care and alone time isn't an option because there are so many things to do. I know I must divide my time up to care for five other people, in addition to our congregation, plus extended family and friends. But if I don't take time to breathe, meditate, and regroup, I will not survive.

There is power and restoration in your retreat. It was in my quiet moments that God revealed the purpose of this journey. It was in my quiet moments where I was able to refuel my mind and regain my joy. It was in my quiet moments where I snatched my identity back. It was in my quiet moments where I gained the confidence to tell this story.

I was able to overcome the insecurities of being vulnerable. Although I am surrounded by my village and have had support, the breakthrough happened in moments where it was just me and God. I am surviving because He is holding me up. And He's holding you as well.

THE SACRIFICE.

The doctors would often tell me that they didn't know which would have been easier; finding out about Evan's issues while I was pregnant or finding out after he was born. I'm not certain if the anxiety and stress would have changed. In my opinion, I felt that it was easier knowing beforehand because at least I was able to prepare my mind that a storm was coming.

Even though I was prepared, I remember being so angry with God. I didn't fully understand how He orchestrated things. I did grow up in church and know plenty of scriptures, so I knew that there was a time and place for everything. Eccelsiates 3:1-8 states *"for everything there is a season, and a time for every purpose under heaven: a time to be born, and a time to die; a time to plant, and a time to pluck up that which is planted; a time to kill, and a time to heal; a time to break down, and a time to build up; a time to weep, and a time to laugh; a time to mourn, and a time to dance; a time to cast away stones, and a time to gather stones together; a time to embrace, and a time to refrain from embracing; a time to seek, and a time to lose; a time to keep, and a time to cast away; a time to rend, and a time to sew; a time to keep silence, and a time to speak; a time to love, and a time to hate; a time for war, and a time for peace"*.. But I couldn't understand for the life of me why God would make my dreams come true and then snatch them out from in front of me so quickly.

I thought it was perfect. I was a gymnast, dancer, and cheerleader my entire life. I performed in the Aloha Bowl in Hawaii on Christmas Day, I danced in all my high school musicals. I choreographed for my church's choir performance for Verizon's How Sweet the Sound, which we won nationally in 2010. I have performed at the Los Angeles Clippers game halftime shows, the Los Angeles Sparks game, Six Flags Magic Mountain, and at Disney World in Orlando. I was an All-American cheerleader. I have praise danced across the city and nation. All I ever wanted was my own dance studio.

It was practically handed to me. All I had to do was pay the rent. The owners had built this beautiful space in the heart of Compton, California. It had mirrors and a top-of-the-line sound system. There was a waiting area for parents (with a window where they would have been able to peak through to check on their children). I had customers lined up ready to sign their children up.

When I was five months pregnant, I had an amazing launch concert with a Production Team that was second to none. What I didn't have was a game plan for getting pregnant during this time with a child with health challenges that required lots of doctors' visits. And since the studio was new, I didn't have time to get an LLC, or hire a staff to help me while I was away. I lost money, I lost clients, and eventually, I lost my momentum.

After Evan got on his feet, I begged the owners to let me come back and try again. I didn't have the money to pay them, but they let me come back for a second chance and then, boom, Evan went right back into the hospital. I gave up after that. The reality was just that with all that he needed; I couldn't even focus on the studio. I couldn't plan concerts. I was no longer organized.

The definition of sacrifice is the act of giving up something that you want to keep especially in order to get or do something else or to help someone. I didn't only sacrifice my dance studio; I sacrificed my job and career. I sacrificed my emotions, and my time with family and friends.

In 2016 Evan was two years old and Elijah was about six months old. I couldn't accept any jobs that my Project Coordinator was trying to assign me to. Either Evan had a doctor's appointment scheduling conflict or sometimes I would wake up and think I was going to work, and we ended up in the ER because he was struggling to breathe.

I had to take a reduction in hours because I became unreliable. It had gotten so bad that they offered me a position where I no longer worked for them as a full-time employee but could be an on call Independent Contractor. Then I would be able to just go to work when I was available. It sounded good but wasn't the best overall when it came to me having to lose my benefits because at the time, it was my health insurance that covered the rest of my family. This meant that I would no longer be able to invest money into my 401k for my retirement, and my nice-sized involuntary life insurance policy would be gone.

I talked it over with my husband and we really had to decide what would be best. I was grateful for the longevity of my job. I had been there for thirteen years

They knew I was a good worker. They knew I was loyal, and the situation was that I had encountered a season where my family became my priority over my job. So, they gave me an option that would benefit them and me. I don't think another company would have done that. Or maybe they only did it because I had invested the years. I made the decision to become an on call Independent Contractor. Things did become easier as far as the obligation of going to work and being available for the jobs scheduled, but it was a sure shift in our finances.

I sacrificed my emotions. I was a first-time mom. I was supposed to be so happy and cheerful. I tried to press through the emotions, but I never could get it together. Even now, there is a sense of guilt that surfaces from time to time, when I see him suffering and I must ask myself if I made the right decisions. When we go to the doctor's office or for small procedures and he flips out because he fears needles and he yells at me and tells me I'm tricking him or that it's my fault that he is in pain. I have to be laser focused and know that it's out of hurt and pain and that he doesn't mean it because he doesn't fully understand how we fought to make the best decisions we could for him. I think how just a little needle stick is nothing compared to what he endured at 2 weeks old and how we made so many decisions to save his life.

One day I'll be able to explain it to him but in the meantime, I need to remain strong and not let him see my hurt, pain and my invisible scars and damage from this storm. As moms we already endure so many days of guilt where we ask ourselves, *"Am I doing this right? Did I do that right? Am I living up to my ancestor's expectations?"*

And don't get me started on all the "professional" moms on social media. They are packing lunches and laying out clothes in totes for each day of the week. My daily goal is to make it through with no trips to the ER. I'm just trying to keep everyone alive in my family.

There are times we sacrifice going to events and friends' houses because Evan can't get sick. If the wind is blowing too hard or it's super cold, we can't leave the house. For us, leaving means we could potentially spend the next week in the hospital because he can't fight the flu or virus that he caught.

In those years where we had to thicken his juice, I would have to hide goody bags from birthday parties because he would cry his little eyes out when I took the Capri Sun juice out. He didn't understand that he couldn't drink regular liquids. Some adults didn't understand either. They would say *"oh he doesn't need that"* or *"it's nasty"*, and *"he doesn't want it"*, like it was an option. It was irritating because I would think to myself, *I don't have time to explain to you the reason why we must do this.* We didn't just decide to start thickening his liquid on our own. It was medically necessary because his windpipe won't close, which allows liquid to go down the wrong pipe, causing a build-up of fluid on his lungs.

Now to the average two-year-old, it may not be a big deal, but to Evan who has a heart condition which affects his immune system and who isn't strong enough to fight off pneumonia, it's very necessary. Those were risks we just weren't ready to take. At the end of the day, it's us sitting in the hospital bedside watching him fight for his life.

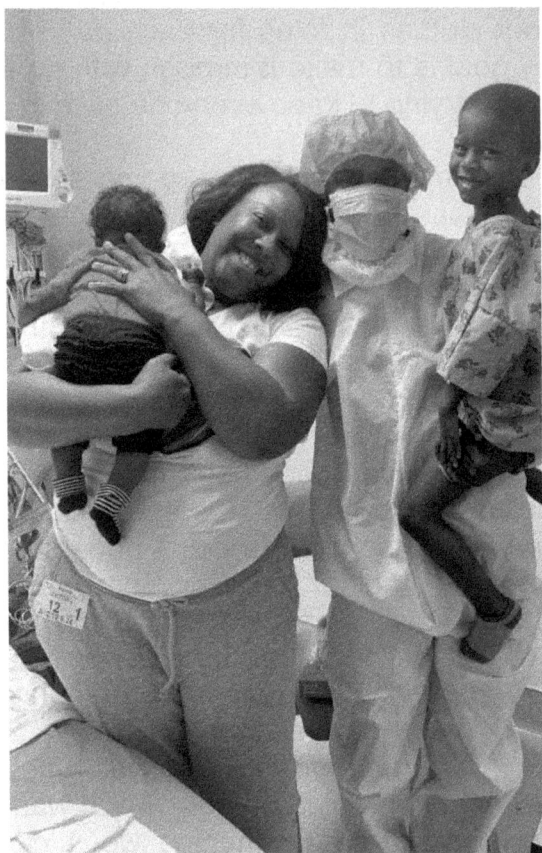

THE SUPERNATURAL.

The name Evan means "Little Warrior" in American and "God is gracious" in Hebrew. But it wasn't until after Evan was born that I googled the meaning of his name. I don't believe in coincidence, but I do believe in discernment and the Holy Spirit. There is no doubt in my mind that God wasn't walking side by side with us this entire journey. There were many moments I couldn't tap in and pray for myself when I was knee deep in the storm, but it's amazing how the biblical stories and scriptures can rise up in your spirit.

I remembered the story of Job and how he didn't do anything wrong, but God allowed Satan to strip everything from him. *"Though he slay me, yet will I trust in him: but I will maintain mine own ways before him"* Job 13:15. When it all first began, I wasn't sure why God allowed us to go through this or how He would bring us out. But I trusted in Him every step of the way. After I got tired of asking God why, I read through Job's story and was reminded that in the end Job received double for his trouble. For every time I cried, I was reminded that Psalms 30:5 says *"weeping may endure for a night, but joy cometh in the morning."* There were a lot of nights that I cried but when it was over, God blessed us with some favor that we know we didn't deserve.

In 2016, we sought out to purchase our first home. After moving back in with my parents, and sacrificing, we were able to watch our home be built all from the ground up. This was not a part of our plan. We were in search of a "fixer upper" and just like that God worked it out.

During every surgery while waiting in the waiting room trying not to allow anxiety to consume me, I was reminded of Philippians 4:6 *"Do not be anxious about anything, but in every situation, by prayer and petition, with thanksgiving, present your requests to God. And the peace of God, which transcends all understanding, will guard your hearts and your minds in Christ Jesus."* Everyone always wondered how I was able to be so calm and at peace during his procedures. It was because of that scripture.

I would tell God exactly what was on my heart and in my mind. Of course, He is all-knowing, but He likes to hear it from us. I was speaking it into existence. I would speak peace; I would speak victory and I would speak healing over my storm. In moments where it seemed like Evan wouldn't get healed, I was reminded of James 5:14-16 *"Is anyone among you sick? Let them call the elders of the church to pray over them and anoint them with oil in the name of the Lord. And the prayer offered in faith will make the sick person well; the Lord will raise them up. If they have sinned, they will be forgiven"* I was prideful about a lot of things, but i was never ashamed to call on the elders of the church to pray for my child. Still to this day, I know when to reach out for an extension in my prayer line.

When the load became so heavy for me to carry, I was reminded about 1 Peter 5:7 *"Casting all your care upon him; for he careth for you."* We get so caught up in the storms, that we forget God's power and how He loves us.

That storm was too big for me to ride out on my own. I had to place it at His feet. Worship carried me through. I would often suffer in silence and then I was reminded of a later verse in that same chapter of 1 Peter which states *"but the god of all grace, who hath called us unto his eternal glory by Christ Jesus, after that ye have suffered a while, make you perfect, stablish, strengthen, settle you."*

The amount of strength and peace I have gained in this storm is beyond me. God has been so gracious and so kind in sustaining me. I could have lost my mind in some of those storm pockets. But He kept me! When I was tired of watching my baby suffer and thoughts would rise that I was the only mom that ever had to endure this type of storm, I am reminded of Mary, the mother of Jesus. In my opinion she endured the biggest storm any mother could face. She watched her son be crucified to save mankind. Her testimony is still being told generations later. I have kept that story in my back pocket the entire time I've been enduring this storm. It encourages me that if one mom can make it through, then I know that I am not by myself. Another mom or another friend may need to hear my story or your story one day.

Recently, one of my best friends dialed me by accident. When I picked up the phone, I could hear the ambulance in the background asking her what happened. She calmly explained to the paramedics how her daughter was choking and went limp as she was driving. I stayed on the phone the entire time thinking this is it.

This is my calling. I'm a pro at 911 calls. I'm also an *ER Mom Specialist*. I know how to remain calm and can talk another mom off of the ledge.

I was praying as I continued to listen to her conversation with the medic team. I thought she was going to get on the phone with me after they guided her off the freeway. But to my surprise, she hung up on me. Funny thing is, she called me by accident and neither one of us knew. However, I interpreted that moment as a proud friend that my spirit was needed for that moment. I was able to text her after and say, *"Mom, you did good. You did everything right. Don't let guilt rise up in you because you did everything you were supposed to do".* I overheard the paramedics telling her never to pull over on the freeway because she could get sideswiped. But she did what any mom would do, which is fight or flight, sink or swim.

When your child is sick, you react with impulse. You're thinking, *how can I save my child?* That's all that matters. When I sit with my now 7yr old miracle child, I am reminded that this journey was never about me. It doesn't matter how many times I cry or ask God why my child? The truth is, this story is written to share with another mom who one day may be in my shoes. Your story may be different from mine.

Maybe you are a single mother; you may have lost a child to tragedy or maybe your child is in and out of prison or on and off drugs, maybe in and out of the courtroom. People always say we are in the same boat, but I'd like to rephrase this and say, *"We are all in the same storm, just sailing in different boats."*

Clouds may be different, but the rainbow at the end are always the same colors. Still, I have not found a pot of gold at the end of any rainbow. Which brings me to this point. Quite frankly, my storm is nowhere near over. But the number of mommies that I've helped along the way has brought so much joy to my heart. It may be so dark and gloomy now, but I promise you that *the storm you are facing is worth the testimony*.

A WORD FROM MY

HUSBAND

Let me start by declaring how proud I am of my wife for publishing her first book. I was able to witness the late nights and hard work to finish this book. With all that we have going on in our home with 3 small children and ministry, she was committed to completing this book.

Our journey with our son Evan has been incredibly challenging. What had begun as the joy of starting a family, turned into a nightmare that we just could not wake up from. I remember the joy I felt when we found out my wife was pregnant. We both were super excited and then we received the call that would change our lives.

We were at home relaxing when the call came in from the genetics counselor informing us that there was a red flag in the blood work and that we needed to come into the office the next week for them to explain the findings. Of course, being a concerned father, I told my wife we were not going to wait all the way until the next week. So, we jumped in the car and headed to the genetics counselor's office with our emotions all over the place.

As I sat down in the office and listened to the report, my heart fell out of my chest and the pain I felt was so unbearable. At the time, we lived nearly an hour away from the doctor's office, so that was an awkward ride home. After arriving home, we prayed, and both began to cry. As the husband, I wanted to be strong for my wife but as a father, I could not hold back my tears.

The genetics counselor suggested that we abort the baby and just try again since we were both still young. But after praying about the matter, we decided that we were going to trust God and have the baby. My wife was only 3 months pregnant at this time so for the next several months my nerves were bad, my anxiety was high, but I remained hopeful.

This was our first child together, so it should have been an exciting moment for us, but there wasn't a lot of excitement and it was hard for me to just enjoy the whole pregnancy. The thought of my son being born and was going to be facing multiple issues including severe heart problems and down syndrome was breaking my heart every day. I was angry with God because I felt that this was unfair for my wife and I to have to go through this. Watching people that were not married having healthy babies and people that didn't even want kids having healthy babies really bothered me. I felt that because I was a Pastor that has been faithful to God for so many years that I should've been exempt from something like this. I just pleaded with God to allow my son to come into this world and live like any other normal kid.

On Christmas Day in 2013, our firstborn son, Evan was born. I stood with my wife the entire time she was in labor and witnessed our son entering the world. I started to feel some relief and some joy once he finally arrived. There were so many doctors and nurses in the room that I was a little concerned, but they also gave me confidence that they were going to do everything at all possible to keep our son alive.

They immediately rushed Evan to the NICU and I followed them closely not wanting to miss anything. He was so tiny and because of the severity of the situation, I wasn't able to hold my son and that really broke my heart. I ran back and forth between seeing Evan and checking on my wife, as she was also having a tough recovery from delivering the baby.

The very next day after Evan was born, they stabilized him enough to move him across the street from Sunset Kaiser to Children's Hospital. The paramedic driver and doctor told me to meet them across the street, but I just jumped in the ambulance with them because I refused to ever leave Evan's side. Once we arrived across the street to Children's Hospital, we were greeted by quite a few doctors and nurses to get him settled in as they strategized how to get him to surgery and bring him out successfully.

At this point, I'm running back and forth from Kaiser checking on my wife and Children's hospital checking on Evan. I felt a little better, but I was still very concerned because Evan needed to have heart surgery immediately, but he was underweight, so they had to wait until he gained a little more weight.

After meeting with the surgeons, they informed us that they were going to have to go through with the heart surgery even though he was under weight and it was a possibility that there could be complications during the surgery and the possibility that he wouldn't make it through the surgery, but we put it in God's hands and sat back waiting for a miracle.

As we patiently waited for Evan to come out of surgery, I begged and pleaded with God to save his life and allow us to take him home. By the grace of God, he made it through the surgery, but after a few days, we were informed that Evan would need a pacemaker, so he had to go back into surgery. In all my years of living, I've never needed to use my faith like this. So, this journey with Evan has increased my faith. For the next 37 days, we had to live at Children's Hospital and slept on a small couch in Evan's hospital room.

During this time, I tried to remain strong for my wife but on the inside, I was mentally and emotionally drained and went to the car a few times throughout the day to just cry. Through this entire process, I still preached every Sunday at our church and taught bible study every Wednesday night. The board at the church encouraged me to take off as long as I needed to so that I could deal with my son, but they didn't understand that preaching was not only my assignment, but it was also my therapy.

Preaching Through my pain helped me during this process. After preaching I would jump back in my car and cry all the way back to the hospital. I just wanted our son to be healed and for this storm to be over. I saw what it was doing to my wife every day and it hurt my heart to see her also mentally and emotionally drained. There were days that I didn't know what to say to her, so I would just hug her really tight and let her cry on me. I would wake up in the middle of the night at the hospital and she would be standing next to Evan's bed just holding his hand and I would immediately start praying for her strength. I realized that it was draining both of us.

One thing that stood out during this time at the hospital was how many mothers that were on the same floor dealing with a sick child with no support from their husbands or child's father. The fathers that did show up, we all bonded and encouraged each other. I tip my hat off to every father that can understand the importance of being there for their child that's dealing with health challenges and to be a support system for the mother of the child. I made sure that every morning that Evan woke up that he saw my face and I spent a lot of time by his bedside. For every surgery, I walked alongside his bed as they rolled him into surgery and stayed while they prepped him. Children are blessed to have great mothers that would do anything for their child but it's a double blessing to have a praying and supportive father.

Storms like this can test the strength of a marriage and I'm blessed that our marriage survived this storm. There were days dealing with all of this that we would be a little moody and snap at each other over small things, but overall, our love for each other increased and allowed us to see how important it was for us to pray together. Of course, sleeping in the hospital we couldn't be intimate but holding hands in the elevator, going downstairs to the cafeteria to eat dinner for date night, watching movies on the laptop, and having our little talks meant everything to me. I'm grateful that I have a relationship with God because that's the only thing that kept me through this.

As a man, I take a lot of pride in trying to be the best father that I can be to all my children. So, watching our son Evan go through so much so early and not being able to do anything for him, it broke me so bad, all I could do was just turn it all over to God. And He kept performing miracles and giving me strength. There were days that I thought I was going to lose my mind, but God held me together.

At first, I couldn't believe that God would allow this to happened to me. but then God showed me that He would use us to show other parents how to get through these types of storms. Our faith was on display and we couldn't make God look bad. When I look back at this journey with Evan, I thank God every day for keeping our son through it all. Unfortunately, other kids went through the same problems as Evan and did not survive. But by the grace of God, our son, Evan is still here.

Elton Johnson

ACKNOWLEDGEMENTS

This journey has been one for the books (pun intended). I'm so humbled and grateful that the Lord chose me and trusted me with the task of being Evan's Mom. God, I thank you for being a keeper and for sustaining my mind during such a storm. I hope I didn't let you down.

My dear EJ!! My husband, & my Pastor, thank you for walking under this umbrella with me and for holding the umbrella when my arms got weak. Thank you for believing in me and pushing me to complete this book. None of this would be possible without my teammate. You are one of a kind. I Love You!

To Trent, Evan, Elijah, & Charlee B: We sacrificed so much in this storm and for this project. Thank you for allowing Mommy the time to get it done. I hope you all know how much Mommy loves you. This book is for us!!! #JPartyOf6

Mom and Dad, thank you both for instilling determination and perseverance in me. Thank you for teaching me how to shoot for the stars. Because of you I have taken the limits off of my dreams and goals. Thank you for riding it out with us at the hospital. I love you and there aren't enough words to tell you Thank you for all you've done in my life.

My one and only big bro, Charles Loray....BRO, I MADE IT!!!! WE MADE IT!!! With God on our side, our reach is endless. You are the best uncle ever and I love you so much!! Jan, you have taught me so much. I love you sis!

Michelle Collins, you are an angel walking on earth. Everyone needs a mentor and life coach as dedicated, committed, and consistent as you.

Dominique Lewis, you are so much more than an assistant. THANK YOU!! THANK YOU! THANK YOU.

To all of my aunts, uncles and cousins, thank you for your support and prayers. (RIP Uncle John)

To the Metropolitan Baptist Church, Los Angeles: Thank you for being patient with me and praying me through a tough time. #ButGod will always be our Metro Insider.

Honorable mentions:
The Wades (Pop, Mom, Sue & Syd), Jawane & Shonta Hilton, Shep & Shalonda Crawford, Pastor Xavier L. Thompson, Curtis and Jennifer Lollis, Kenny Clark, Anthony Chambers, Deon Lewis, my staff then and now, Darnell & Kiara Manuel, LaMicha Williams, Dr. Timothy Degner, "7Sent", Monique Harris, Wanda Scott, Denise Houston, Kimberly Bolden, LaKeisha Keith, FACS, Team Evan, and all of our friends, too many to mention individually, who prayed near and far.

ABOUT THE AUTHOR

Charlé Q. Johnson is a wife, mother of 3, and a ray of sunshine to everyone she comes into contact with. She is the First Lady of The Metropolitan Baptist Church where her husband Elton L. Johnson is the Pastor, and currently serves as the Overseer of the Women's Ministry, Chief of Staff, & Event Producer.

"Lady Charlé" as she's affectionately called, enjoys dancing, mentoring young girls, and spending time with her family. She is an advocate for creating environments that encourage, embrace, and edify women. When Lady Charlé is not working with women, you can find her traveling the city with her Praise Dance Ministry "Chosen II Conquer".

She is also known as one of the choreographers for the "Verizon Wireless 2010 How Sweet the Sound" National Winners, Voices of Destiny.

And as overcomer, her biggest challenge was navigating the health complexities of her firstborn son, Evan. She has empathy for mothers who have children with various challenges and uses her own journey and process as a testimony.

www.sharlayquiana.com

Facebook: Sharlay Quiana
Instagram: @SharlayQuiana

For more information or bookings:
info@sharlayquiana.com

133